P9-CSH-432

LIFELINE:

THE RELIGIOUS UPBRINGING

OF YOUR CHILDREN

LIFELINE:

THE RELIGIOUS UPBRINGING
OF YOUR CHILDREN

James B. Stenson

Scepter Publishers

Princeton, NJ

Books by James B. Stenson

— *Upbringing: A Discussion Handbook for Parents of Young Children*

— *Lifeline: The Religious Upbringing of Your Children*

— *Preparing for Adolescence: Answers for Parents*

— *Preparing for Peer Pressure: A Guide for Parents of Young Children*

— *Successful Fathers*

Available from Scepter Publishers
(800) 322-8773 or www.scepterpublishers.org

Library of Congress Cataloging-in-Publication Data

Stenson, James B
    Lifeline : the religious upbringing of your children / James B. Stenson.
        p.   cm.
    Includes bibliographical references and index.
    ISBN 0-933932-97-9 (pbk. : alk. paper)
    1. Parenting--Religious aspects--Catholic Church. 2. Children--Religious life. I. Title.
BX2352.S74   1996
248.8'45--dc20   96–44708
                                                            CIP

First printing   February 1997
Eighth printing   October 2002

ISBN 0-933932-97-9

© 1996 James B. Stenson
Printed in the United States of America

Contents

Introduction

Dear Friend,

A parent of small children has little time to spare, so I have made this book fairly short and straight to the point. *Lifeline* presents you with practical advice and earnest encouragement for raising your children to become level-headed, courageous, responsible Christian adults who honor you and God all their lives.

The book also gives you clear principles and high but attainable ideals for your family life, insights that can lead you to take effective action with your children now, while you still have time. *Lifeline* should lead you, above all, to *think*. Serious reflection about your mission and your children's future will give you *purposeful direction* for your family life, and this will embolden you to *plan* and to *act* effectively.

Nothing in your life is more important than this, and you do not have much time.

Here is a crucial principle, an inexorable fact of life, that all parents must understand: You have one chance, and only one, to raise your children right.

If you succeed in this, your life's greatest responsibility, your children will bring you honor and happiness for as long as you live. Years from now, they will live as competent, responsible, confident adults who are committed to live by Christian principles. Each of them will be respected as a man or woman of conscience and character, faithful to the religious convictions you taught them. Each will marry someone who shares your family's principles—and that marriage will be permanent, stable, and happy. Each will present you with grandchildren who will be the delight of your later years, a great reward for your life of sacrificial service to your family.

For more than twenty years as an educator, I had the experience of knowing parents who led their children to grow up this way. I came to know their family lives intimately, and I learned from them. Though all these parents had ups and downs through their children's growing years—victories and reverses, triumphs and trials, with many doubts along the way—in the end they succeeded: their children finally grew to become outstanding Christian men and women.

This book succinctly explains how they did it. I pass their experiences along to you as advice and encouragement. If you are like so many other young parents today, you need all the support you can get—for reasons that will be explained within.

I must warn you here at the outset, though, that raising children well is challenging. That means it is hard work. It takes relentless dedication and passionate love and reliance on God's all-powerful help.

So please set aside any ideas you may have that this book will make your present life any easier. Raising children right is a full-time commitment, and then some; there is no such thing as a hassle-free home.

There seems to be a kind of economic law in child-raising: You either pay now or you pay later.

If you struggle now to surpass yourself, to direct all your powers toward developing the character and conscience of your children while they still live with you, then later you will reap the rewards. By the time your children reach their late teens, they will be exceptional Christian adults. Then you can rest, and enjoy peace of mind, as you see them live by what you taught them.

Yours will not be the sad experience of so many other parents—those who neglect their children's upbringing in youth and spend the rest of their lives regretting it.

It works like this, you see: Character and faith are *formed* in children. They do not just appear spontaneously and unaided as children grow in age. Parents who work at this, and who know what they are doing, manage to form these and other strengths in their children. But parents who practice ongoing neglect—through misdirection or inertia—see their children grow older without ever growing up. Their children get stuck in childish self-centeredness, a never-ending adolescence; though they may pull down a decent salary as adults, their personal lives and marriages are a wreck.

All children acquire habits and attitudes in family life every single day. This dynamic goes on constantly at home whether parents are aware of it or not, whether they direct it or not. But which habits? Which attitudes? This is the core question.

Conscientious parents work untiringly to turn the habits into virtues and the attitudes into conscience. Other parents let matters slide, counting on time alone to turn their kids around; this is a mistake, but they learn it too late.

There it is, the choice that faces parents today: Pay now or pay later. . . . Form your children well, or just let them be. Lead them to strong character and faith, or just keep them amused with an endless stream of pleasant sensations. Raise them as producers, or school them as consumers. Form their moral conscience, or let them be led by their passions and appetites. Teach them your religious faith as a rule of life, or let them grow up living as if God does not exist.

And the consequences of those choices are what parents see later in their children's lives. . . . Adults who live as responsible Christians, or as technically skilled barbarians. Confident happiness in life, or substance abuse and promiscuity. Stable and happy family lives, or marriages broken apart. Well formed and confident grandchildren, or wounded and lonely grandchildren—or even no grandchildren at all.

Along with all this, the final consequence of our choices: heaven or hell.

Ask any professional who deals with troubled adults and shaky marriages. Talk with any priest, marriage counselor, clinical psychologist or psychiatrist. All of them will tell you: the problems stem from childhood, and they begin at home.

I tell you all this so you can steel yourself for the task ahead, once you see the outline of this great challenge and learn what you can do about it. What is at stake for you is nothing less than the earthly and eternal happiness of your children. Nothing is more important than this.

You can draw courage from knowing that God is with you. When he gave you your children, he gave you a sacred mission in life—and he, who began this good work in you, will bring it to completion. This he has promised.

So we begin this work by reflecting on your mission. . . .

James B. Stenson
Chestnut Hill, MA

1

Mission

GOD, IN ALL HIS INFINITE WISDOM and love, has called each of us here on earth to carry out some purpose of his, some divine mission that contributes, mysteriously, to his grand design for the redemption of mankind. He calls each of us, every single one of us, to eternal life—to an everlasting happiness with him, a joy and peace infinitely surpassing our most ambitious imaginings, the breathtaking bliss of children united at last, and forever, with their Father.

God loves us as his children. To ransom us from evil, to save each of us from the "second death" (Revelation 2: 11), he sent us his only begotten Son to become one of us, to live like us on earth, and to offer bloody sacrifice for our salvation. Jesus Christ, both God and man, became united with us so that we would become one with him for all eternity. In his love, he remains with us in the Eucharist and in his Mystical Body, the Church. He has called each of us to return his love by carrying out our mission—to love God above all things and to serve him by serving those around us, beginning with our family, and radiating outward to all those other souls whose lives he has Providentially intertwined with our own.

God has called each of us to be a saint. And he has called you, a parent, to a special divine mission. He has entrusted you and your beloved spouse with children, the offspring of your love for each other and his love for your family.

From all eternity he has ordained that you should serve him by leading your children to love and serve him with all their heart and soul and mind and strength—so that they and you will win eternal life and that hundred-fold of happiness here on earth which he has promised to all who love him.

This is why God has put you on earth. This is why he has sent you your children. Their earthly and eternal happiness is your mission, and you will not know true peace or joy unless you embrace this mission as your greatest responsibility, and surpass yourself in its fulfillment. But if you do embrace this vocation, if you love God and your children to the point of sacrifice, the way Jesus Christ taught and did, you will never know an end to your happiness.

Vision

God has called you—you, personally—from all eternity to lead your children to happiness. This sacred calling is so important that we should dwell on it a while here, seek out its implications, so that you can undertake it with clearer vision and stronger courage. Like all those figures in Scripture who received a divine mission, you need vision and courage, which are the offspring of faith, hope, and love.

Perhaps you remember an incident from your childhood, as many people do, when you first looked up at the night-time sky and wondered at the sparkling array of stars flung across the blackness. Your young mind strained to grasp their vast antiquity and distance from earth. You gazed at the endless void beyond and, with swelling awe, grappled with the mystery and power of the terms *infinite, endless, forever and ever.*

To grasp the true nature of your divine parental mission, its awesome beauty and holiness, you should return to that insight you had as a small child.

Reflect on your life's calling like this: When God first formed the universe eons ago, when he first shaped the blazing stars out of nothing, he thought of you.

He fashioned you in his infinite mind, and he foresaw everything about you. He saw the tangle of circumstances that make up your life, every detail of your destiny from conception to death, your threaded part in his tapestry of human history, the interweaving of your life with the souls of others—your forebears and parents, your teachers and friends, your spouse, your children and their own destiny.

Every particle of your life, past and present and to come, existed in the mind of God when the universe was still a lifeless void. He loved you then, and loves you now, more than you love your own children.

And God has loved your children from all eternity. His eternal plan for their destiny—that they should freely love him here on earth and forever—requires *you* as his loving, self-sacrificing instrument. He calls upon you, in all the circumstances of your family life, to unite your heart and mind and will to his own, so that your whole family will love and serve him here on earth and in heaven for all eternity.

You can better understand your sacred mission, the salvation of your children, their happiness on earth and in heaven, by looking ahead as well. See it this way. . . .

At this time in history, the turn of the 21st century, all the great cities of the world are splendid with man-made structures of stone and glass that soar skyward, wondrous achievements of human ambition and ingenuity. But someday they, too, will fall. In several thousand years, cities like New York and London and São Paulo will lie in rubble; they will suffer the fate of other places in antiquity—Nineveh, Babylon, Antioch, Nicaea, and other sites celebrated in Scripture, now gone forever.

When today's great cities are no more, when the passage of time has worn them to flattened earth, the souls of your children will still *be*. Your children's souls are forever.

Where will your children's souls be? This question should haunt you, press on you daily, drive you to surpass your limitations. Your children will exist for all eternity in one of only two states: everlasting happiness with God in heaven, or everlasting pain and sorrow in hell. Your children will freely live and die in God's friendship—or they will freely cut themselves off from his love while they live, and then suffer the "second death" for all eternity.

You, as a loving parent, must never lose sight of this horrendous threat to your children. There is a hell. Hell exists, and all its evil forces are poised at the souls of your children. Our blessed Savior warned of hell repeatedly, more than a dozen times in the Gospels (see Matthew 3: 10-12; 8: 11-12; 10: 27-28; 12: 32-33; 16: 26; 22: 14; 25: 32-33, 41-46; Mark 3: 29; 9: 42-48; Luke 3: 9-17; 16: 22-31; John 3: 36; 8: 21-24,

34-35). He warned each of us, all of us, of the dreadful fate awaiting those who reject his love and forgiveness.

He calls upon you, as his loving servant, to save your children and lead them to him. He calls on you to love your children as he loves them, to the point of sacrifice.

Love is not just a sentiment, an emotional state. In a real sense, love *is* sacrifice. Love is the willingness and ability to endure and overcome obstacles, setbacks, disappointments, tedium—any hardship whatsoever—for the sake of someone's welfare and happiness. Love is another term for *responsibility*.

God calls every parent to responsibility. He will hold you answerable for the eternal destiny of your children. After your death, when you pass to judgment, he will ask you: "How well did you teach our children—yours and mine—to know me, to love me, and to serve me?" You and your spouse must be able to reply: "We did the very best we could. . . ."

That is what God asks of you, to do the very best you can. If you ask him, he will supply the rest, whatever you need to surpass your shortcomings. As he said through the angel Gabriel: "Nothing is impossible to God."

Heartfelt devotion

In the Scriptures we see that every divine vocation involves undertaking some great challenge, some seemingly impossible problem.

We see Abraham, Moses, Joshua, Samuel, David, the Maccabees, the great prophets, and so many other men and

women—all given some great responsibility, apparently insol-
uble, to prepare the way for the Promised One, the
Redeemer.

Then, once he came and redeemed us, his disciples
received the same great calling to responsibility. Peter, John
and all the other apostles, Stephen, Paul, Timothy, the con-
verts mentioned in the Acts and the Epistles, and the generations of saints who succeeded them up to our era—all
received God's calling, his command to go forth, to teach, to
baptize, to "turn the hearts of fathers to their children, and
the unbelieving to the wisdom of the just . . . to prepare for
the Lord a perfect people" (Luke 1: 17).

He calls each Christian parent to the same mission. He
calls upon you to undertake the greatest challenge of your
life, the salvation of your children.

You, like all these other people called by God, may at first
react with the same emotional response they felt—a shrinking
back in dread, a profound anxiety. To take on great responsibility nearly always provokes fear. Abraham, Moses, and David
knew fear. So did Peter and Paul and the others. Paul spoke
specifically of his "daily pressing anxiety." Indeed even Christ
himself, in his holy human nature, sweat blood in the garden
of Gethsemane when confronted with the momentous climax
of his mission.

You, too, when you really grasp the seriousness and magnitude of your parental vocation, may sense the same anxiety
in the face of your enormous responsibility—your responsibility to shape your children's character and conscience for
life, to lead them toward lifelong greatness and then to eternal life.

Part of your uneasiness or fear may derive from perception of your unworthiness, your lack of adequate preparation for parenthood, or your own inadequate religious upbringing.

This perception may indeed be true. In the wake of nearly every great ecumenical council in history, a time of confusion has followed, a period marked by pride, resistance to authority, outright disobedience, struggles for power, and seriously flawed catechetical teaching. Over the past generation, we have lived through such an era, and it may have done you harm.

Through no fault of your own, you may have been uninstructed or poorly formed in faith, maybe even in moral standards as well. In place of Christ's doctrine, developed and refined through the centuries by his Church, your teachers may have taught you a pop sociology or ideological cant, something other than the truth about eternal life.

When you were in your mid-teens, with your growing mind ready to grasp the intellectual basis for your family's faith, the loving belief that sustained your family line for centuries, you may have been led into trivial activism—pasting up collages, swaying to and singing folk songs, and other playground diversions. You may not have been taught what your forebears were taught about God's love and sacrifice, his teachings and warnings, his sacraments, and your eternal vocation.

You may not have been taught right from wrong, and so you may have done wrong—as you now know. As you look back on your childhood and youth, you may have regrets for what you did, or failed to do, thus offending God.

All this—your past and present faults, your yawning gaps of religious instruction, your lapses, your uncertainty of faith may cause you worry, even anxiety, when you look upon your children and realize the great task God has set before you. Where will you find the faith and strength to serve your family as God wants?

Take courage from God. Over and over again in the Scriptures, God says to his chosen servants what he says now to you: *Do not be afraid.*

From all eternity, he had you and your children in mind when he said: "Fear not, for I have redeemed you; I have called you by name: you are mine" (Isaiah 43: 2).

God had you and your parental vocation in mind when he said: "Do not be afraid. I am the first and the last, the one who lives. Once I was dead, but now I am alive forever and ever. I hold the keys to death and the netherworld" (Revelation 1: 17-18).

His love for you and your children should give you courage to endure and overcome anything: "There is no fear in love, but perfect love drives out fear. . . . We love because he first loved us" (I John 4: 18-19).

He has promised he will never let you down: "God is faithful, and will not let you be tried beyond your strength; but with the trial he will also provide a way out, so that you may be able to bear it" (I Corinthians 10: 13).

To you, his beloved child, whom he has entrusted with beloved children, he counsels through the words of St. Paul: "Be on your guard, stand firm in the faith, be courageous, be strong. Your every act should be done with love" (I Corinthians 16: 13-14).

Christ promised his answer to your prayers for your children: "Ask and it will be given to you; seek and you will find; knock and the door will be opened to you. For everyone who asks, receives; and the one who seeks, finds; and to the one who knocks, the door will be opened. Which one of you would hand his son a stone when he asks for a loaf of bread, or a snake when he asks for a fish? If you then, who are wicked, know how to give good gifts to your children, how much more will your heavenly Father give good things to those who ask him" (Matthew 7: 7-11).

So many times in the Gospel we see Jesus do just this—answer the heartfelt, persistent pleas of parents whose children were in trouble. He raised the little daughter of Jairus to life again (Matthew 9: 18-19, 23-26). He cured the ruler's son (Luke 4: 45-54). He drove the Evil One out of a boy whose tearful father cried out that beautiful prayer, "I do believe; help my unbelief!" (Luke 9: 37-44). He finally answered the relentless, insistent pleas of the Syro-phoenecian mother so filled with faith in his merciful power (Matthew 15: 21-28).

These parents, like you, were normal people who loved their children with all their hearts. They trusted that Jesus would turn his compassionate face to them, direct his power to free their children from a seemingly hopeless calamity. Jesus heard them and answered them. He will hear and answer you, too, if you have faith, as they did, and if you never give up, never lose hope in his all-powerful compassionate mercy.

Have the faith of St. Paul, then, whose inspired words convey God's promise to you: "I am confident of this, that the One who began a good work in you will continue to complete it until the day of Christ Jesus" (Philippians 1: 6).

2

Your Children's Character and Conscience

A GREAT MANY PARENTS TODAY, perhaps through their own weak upbringing, hold mistaken notions about the job of parenthood—and so they and their families meet with frustration, disappointment, and sometimes real tragedy. In your life's experience so far, you have probably known parents like this, maybe even among your siblings and friends.

For you and your children to avoid these problems, you need a clear picture of your task as a parent. Along with this, and related to it, you need to know what mistakes to avoid. And so, in this chapter we will look at the overall job of successful Christian parenthood, and we shall contrast this with the mistaken concepts and approaches that have led to so much pain.

The chapters that follow will spell out details of Christian parental leadership. But first we need to see the job as a whole: what you need to undertake, and why.

Forming character and conscience

Many parents mistakenly believe that their task is to *preserve* character, not *form* it. That is, they believe that children come into the world with beautiful traits, admirable innocence, and that the job of parents is to maintain these as the children grow.

To look at it another way, these misguided parents see their task as mainly keeping children relentlessly busy, always occupied, for "an idle mind is the devil's workshop." Family life is therefore dedicated mainly toward flight from boredom and keeping the children from so-called "bad companions." Parents like this hold the notion, it seems, that their children will somehow grow naturally into fine men and women—if only their childlike qualities can be left intact.

There is some truth to this outlook, of course. There must be, or no one would hold it. Indeed, small children do have some beautiful traits which must be preserved throughout life.

For one thing, once they are instructed in faith, small children have a powerful, beautiful love for God.

They have a powerful love for family, for their parents and brothers and sisters. The most horrifying nightmare for children is to be separated from their family.

They have a love for life itself, a sheer delight in being alive. Each morning, a child awakes to see the day as a gift, an opportunity for fun and accomplishment with family and friends. Work and play are all one, and the child is ever ready for laughter.

And children have a love for the truth. Their gaze on the truth is steady, sometimes startling, and occasionally even embarrassing to adults around them. Small children are incompetent liars; they only learn to lie, to themselves and others, as they grow older.

No question about it, your children should preserve these loves throughout their lives. And they will—*but only if they see them still alive in their parents.* As they grow, children must see their parents still in love with God, their family, life itself, and truth.

Parents can live this way, as we shall later see.

But it is equally clear that children are afflicted with the results of original sin. Alongside the charming traits just mentioned, they are afflicted with serious flaws, faults that grow ever more evident after the age of two, when they begin to say "No" and mean it. They show themselves as fundamentally self-centered creatures, wholly given over to gratifying their appetites and passions, and determined to dominate the lives of those around them by force or manipulation. (Anyone who doubts this should try monitoring a kindergarten playground for a few days; we notice these flaws most clearly, and are appalled by them, in other people's children.)

And we later see these glaring faults in teens and in adults as well. For the simple fact of life's experience is this: If children grow older with these faults uncorrected, then the flaws grow habitual and even monstrous. The kids emerge into adolescence and adulthood as larger versions of what they were in childhood, but with the good traits erased.

Poorly formed children enter adult life as self-centered men and women, driven by appetites and passions and obsessed with domination. Though they may hold good jobs and draw down good salaries, their personal lives are a wreck. They are unprepared for marriage and other serious responsibilities, and they often wind up with broken homes and children out of control.

Sad to say, this family dysfunction—where children grow older but never really grow up—afflicts those families mentioned above, where parents were merely concerned to keep children busy with amusements and counted on the passage of time, somehow, to bring their children to responsible adulthood. Any correction of the children along the way was meant as mere damage-control, directed toward peace and quiet for its own sake and keeping hassles to a minimum.

Misguided parents who raise their children in this way meet frequently with disappointment and heartbreak. They often see their children grow into technically skilled narcissists, people who care for neither their parents nor their own children—if they have any. By way of contrast, these sad considerations lead to your job-description, the task God has called you to.

Your job as a parent is not merely to keep your kids busy and out of trouble. You are not called to make your children's lives little more than an endless series of pleasant sensations, an ongoing apprenticeship in some lifelong drive for power and pleasure.

Your God-given task is this: You are called to spend years in sacrificial effort together with your spouse to lead your children to become competent, responsible, considerate adults who are committed to live by Christian principles all their lives, no matter what the cost.

Your task is to raise adults, not children. Your mission is to form character and conscience within the minds, hearts, and wills of your children. You must work at this ideal every day, without let-up, and see it as your greatest responsibility in life.

Defining character

Let us take a closer look at character. How may we define it?

Character is the sum total of good habits formed in the minds and wills of young people. These habits are called *virtues* or character-strengths. We shall look at them in more detail later, but let's now consider them in outline. The basic Christian virtues are seven in number:

Faith: the belief in God and in all that he has taught us through his Church, including what he teaches about the purpose of human life—that he has made us to know him, love him, and serve him here on earth and to be happy with him forever in heaven.

Hope: the confidence that God watches over us as a loving Father and we therefore have nothing to fear; he will help us through life's great challenges and give us the means for our eternal salvation.

Charity: the love for God above all things whatever, and love for others for his sake; the vision that everyone is a child of God and that we serve him by serving others, our brothers and sisters in the human family.

Sound judgment and conscience (prudence): right reasoning about people, events, ourselves; the ability to make the great distinctions in life—truth from falsehood, good from evil, the beautiful and noble from the squalid.

Responsibility (justice): recognizing and respecting the rights of others, which is the source of our obligations; a sense of duty for the welfare and happiness of others; the willingness and ability to live with the consequences of our free decisions, including our mistakes.

Courageous perseverance (fortitude): the will and ability to overcome or endure problems, not to seek escape; the power to withstand hardship, even physical discomfort and pain, and to rebound from setbacks and disappointments.

Self-mastery (temperance): the ability to say "no" to oneself, to defer or do without gratification; the power to overcome passions and appetites; the habit of enjoying the good things of life in moderation.

This, in summary, is Christian character. It is something real, something attainable by all of us. We know it when we see it in others, and we should want to see it grow within our children's souls.

Building character

How do children acquire these strengths as they grow up? It seems this happens in three ways, and in this order of importance:

First, by *example*: by what the children *witness* in the lives of their parents and other adults whom they admire—for children (like all the rest of us) unconsciously imitate people they admire.

Secondly, by *directed practice*: by what the children are repeatedly *led to do*, or *made to do*, by parents and other respected adults.

Third, by *word*: by *verbal explanation* of what they witness and are led or made to do.

In brief outline, this is a description of your parental vocation.

God calls you to form faith, hope, charity, sound judgment and conscience, a sense of responsibility, courageous perseverance, and self-mastery in your children. And you are to do this by your own purposeful good example, your repeated direction in practice, and your explanations to your children.

To repeat, your teaching must be done in this order, with example in first place. You teach your children most effectively, most deeply, when you are scarcely aware of it—when their sharp eyes are watching you and their busy ears overhear you as you go about living as a responsible Christian adult. To be a good parent, you must first strive to be a good person.

You must also teach the character-strengths through directed practice. You relentlessly lead the children to think and do and say the right thing (for instance, saying *please* and *thank you*), even when nothing seems to be improving within them. You never give up. You maintain confidence that, please God, someday, sooner or later, they will begin to act rightly on their own. You view this persistent daily sacrifice as an investment that will pay off later.

Finally, you teach with your word, but only after you have given good example and directed your children rightly. You know that lectures and scoldings, admonitions and one-on-one talks, have little or no effect on children who fail to see and practice the virtues in family life.

As noted earlier, there seems to be an economic law in children's upbringing: You either pay now or you pay later. Parents who sacrifice to live these virtues themselves, and lead their children to do the same, can later see their children grow into exceptional men and women, the delight of their parents' later lives. But those parents who now live like consumers, who neglect their children's character formation throughout childhood, can spend their later lives in bitter disappointment. This happens all too often. Just look around you.

Someone wise once said: Hard work without some ideal makes life an endless drudgery; but that same hard work, carried out for some passionate ideal, turns life into a grand sporting adventure.

Your life as a parent—indeed, your whole family life itself—can be a sporting adventure once you form and follow that grand passionate ideal that your children grow to become the great men and women whom God envisioned when he entrusted them to your care.

St. Irenaeus once said, "Nothing gives more glory to God than a person who is fully alive."

You and your family will give glory to God when you are filled with God's grace and strive to live a virtuous life. In our urbanized civilization, people seldom find God in nature; the lights of our cities blot out the stars. *If your children do not find God in you, they may never find him at all.*

So set this as your ideal. By the time your children are in their late teens, they should display the great Christian virtues. They should be learned, competent, tough-minded, responsible, nobody's fool or patsy.

At the same time, they should retain all the great loves they had as small children—love for God, love for family, love for life and friends and laughter, and a passionate love for the truth.

With God's help and your vocational dedication, your children will grow to become great men and women, people with the powers of adults and the hearts of children. They will be what Christ called all of us to be: "wise as serpents, and innocent as doves" (Matthew 10: 16). And your family life together will be part of the hundred-fold he promised to those who love and serve him faithfully—a grand and beautiful adventure.

3

Leadership and Discipline

As we have seen, children acquire strong habits of character (that is, the virtues) mostly by example and by directed practice: by what they see and overhear among respected adults, and by what they are led or made to do repeatedly and purposefully.

So the overall strategy of conscientious parents is to lead the children to acquire high, adult-level standards of thinking and behavior. Before the children are out of their teens, they should possess and display the great powers of Christian adulthood: strong religious faith and love (shown in deeds), sound judgment and conscience, personal toughness, and habitual self-discipline. This is what happens, or should happen, in every Christian family.

It is important for you to understand (and pass on to your children as part of their judgment) that every family, including yours, is a society.

This concept is important because it helps you understand your task more clearly and to steel your determination to persevere in it, no matter what.

What is the difference between a mob and a society? It is this.

31

A mob is just a crowd of people without a purpose or leadership or structure. It is just an aimless gathering of people. A society, on the other hand, has three characteristics:

First, a *mission*: a job to accomplish or an aim to attain, which everyone involved understands.

Second, *leadership and a chain of command*: one or more people assume responsibility, and therefore have authority, to direct and teach others in carrying out the overall mission; this implies the right to be obeyed, a right to correct and redirect others lest their mistakes do harm.

Third, *structure*: a clear job description and set of rules (standards of comportment or behavior) so that all of the society's members, at all levels, understand what is expected of them in their efforts to carry out the common mission.

These three elements—mission, leadership, and rules— are found in every successful society, whether a nation, a business, a club, a sports team, or a family. The stronger these elements are, the more successful is the society. A society functions best when it has a clearly important purpose, strong and confident leadership, and a simple but clear set of rules and standards.

This includes your family. You and your spouse do have an extremely important mission—the forming of your children into responsible Christian adults—and this we have seen already. We now turn to consider your leadership role and the standards you have to maintain in family life.

Leadership and discipline

We must make one thing clear here. The word "discipline" does not mean punishment. It sometimes must involve punishment, to be sure, but that is not its main meaning.

"Discipline" is related to the word "disciple" as it is used in the Scriptures and elsewhere, especially in antiquity. It means *teaching* and *leading*. Christ was called "Teacher" (Rabbi, Master) and as such he had disciples. A teacher teaches and his disciples learn. A leader leads and his disciples follow.

Your discipline in the family means, therefore, that you teach and lead your children to understand and to practice responsible Christian adulthood. You teach, they learn. You lead, they follow. Over several years, they learn and follow you until they attain this kind of adulthood themselves.

It follows from this that real discipline (teaching leadership) involves praise and encouragement as well as—even more than—correction and punishment. You teach and lead best when you set high standards for yourself and expect no less from your followers. In any society, including the family, the greatest leaders think and act this way.

It also follows from the above that sometimes correction is necessary, and the best leaders and teachers help their followers learn from their mistakes. (Look in the Gospels and see how Our Lord did this repeatedly with his disciples.) Sometimes, when dealing with young children, you must punish them, and we shall come to this in a moment.

You will find it easier to punish your children, and do
it most effectively, when you think of punishment as *memorable correction*—that is, correction in a matter so important for their welfare that they must remember not to repeat it.

Successful parent-leaders

With this understanding of parental teaching leadership
in mind, let us turn to outline some features of successful
parents. Even in today's troubled world, many parents do succeed in their mission; their children grow up eventually,
sooner or later, to become outstanding, virtuous, and holy
men and women.

There is no such thing, it seems, as a "typical" personal-
ity among such parents. Some, by temperament, are charismatic leaders in all they do, at home or on the job. Others,
by contrast, are quiet and easy-going.

Some seem to sense, intuitively and quickly, what to do
in a host of situations with their children. Others are reflective, far less sure of themselves, and they frequently seek advice from people whose judgment they respect.

Some grew up in stable, happy homes and try to recall
what their parents did right, and then imitate the upbringing they remember from childhood. Others grew up in less
stable homes, even dysfunctional families, but are determined not to repeat the mistakes of their parents.

Most successful parents work in ongoing, unified partnership with their spouses. Others, remarkably, are courageous single parents who manage somehow, with Gods' help, to be both
father and mother to their children. (More on this later.)

In short, one truth seems to stand out: Virtually anyone, any normal man or woman who relies on God and who practices common sense, can be a successful parent. This seems to be the collective experience of human history—and is reason for hope.

Despite these differences of temperament and background and family circumstances, successful parents do have several common approaches to raising children right. There are certain attitudes and practices—but not set formulas—that appear with varying detail again and again in family life. Let us look at these here.

Religious strength

Successful parents *lead* their children to love, honor, and obey God.

The entire family takes their common religious faith seriously and acts upon it to the point of sacrifice. Our relationship with God, like any other truly loving relationship, involves forgetting about our comfort and interests for the sake of someone else's needs and happiness. Love means sacrifice, and sacrifice signifies true love. (The symbol of our Christian faith is the crucifix: Jesus dying on the cross for love of each of us.)

In a Christian family, therefore, prayer and religious practices are not mere formalities or activities carried out from momentum of unreflective habit. On the contrary, prayer is a living part of family life, and our obligations to God, our loving Father, are taken seriously. God lives in the family, not just in church.

In a home like this, children grow to see how conscience (the voice of one's parents) is a lifelong guide for
living right. Conscience is something adults live by, not
just children.

Long-term vision

Inevitably, a Christian outlook on life involves long-
term vision. Parents see their children's eternal destiny as
the end-point of family life and the children's upbringing
within it. Heaven, eternal friendship with God, is the ultimate goal.

Implicit within this vision is a clear picture of the children's life here on earth, how the children will live as adults
in the decades that follow their leaving home. What kind of
men and women will they be?

In any busy family today, parents necessarily struggle
from day to day, week to week, and their vision is often un-
derstandably constricted.

Most of the time, they think ahead only a short distance:
a matter of weeks, maybe a couple of months into the future,
sometimes only as far ahead as next summer or the upcoming school year. Any thoughts of the distant future, twenty or
more years ahead, generally center on considerations of college and career.

Successful parents do not think short-term like this, nor
confine long-term thoughts merely to those of future occu-
pation. They frequently think of their children's future lives
as grown-up men and women, and they think in terms of
character and conscience. They think a great deal about their

children's future marriages, what kind of parents and spouses their children will someday be. They picture their children as adults and ask some serious questions:

- Will our children live as honorable men and women, people of sound character and conscience?

- Will our children be well formed in the virtues of faith, hope, and charity—and sound judgment, a sense of responsibility, courageous perseverance, and self-mastery?

- When confronted with temptation, will they have the conscience and love for God to resist and persevere? And if they fall and do wrong, will they *know* it is wrong and seek God's forgiveness through the sacrament of Reconciliation?

- Will they grow to respect the rights and sensibilities of everyone, without exception, starting with God? Will they habitually practice courtesy and have eyes for the needs of those around them? Will they practice Christian charity, bearing no personal ill will toward anyone, even those who would be their enemies? Will they be ever prepared to apologize, to take initiative in restoring peace and good relations?

- If God calls them to marriage, will each of them form a stable, holy, permanent bond with a spouse who shares our family's principles? Will they pattern their family lives after that of the family they grew up in? Will they present us with grandchildren within whom we can see our values and religious principles still alive?

- If God calls one or more of them to apostolic celibacy, will they live as holy men and women, apostolic and dedicated, embracing souls as their spiritual children who thus become (to our everlasting happiness) our spiritual grandchildren?

- In the world of work, will they be respected for their competence, integrity, and commitment to excellent service? Will they be admired as conscientious professionals, people of honorable ambition—regardless of what they do for a living?

- Will they grow to be confident men and women? Will their confidence come from a clean conscience, living always in the state of grace, a practiced competence, true knowledge of their strengths and shortcomings, and the awareness that they are loved unconditionally by God, family, and friends?

- Will they grow to be great men and women—serious of purpose but light in touch, taking their responsibilities seriously but not themselves? Will they always retain the great loves of childhood: love for God, for family, for life, and for the truth?

In short, successful Christian parents picture a high ideal for their children's growth into maturity. When their sons and daughters are in their late 20's and 30's, they should live as outstanding husbands and wives, mothers and fathers, honorable professionals, great friends, active and responsible citizens.

Great parents earnestly desire that their children grow to outdo them in everything. With this high, long-term ideal before them, they labor each day in guiding, directing, and correcting their children—and, no matter what happens, they never give up.

Unity

Successful parents live *unity*. The husband and wife practice an ongoing partnership, mutually supporting each other, striving to overlook each other's weaknesses, totally committed to serving each other.

Marriage is not a 50–50 proposition. It is more like an 80–20 or 90–10 proposition. That is, each partner *gives* much more than he or she expects in return. Real love does not mean equal sharing; it means serving to the point of sacrifice—forgetting about oneself and giving to serve the needs of others.

Parents who live this way, putting each other in first place, teach great lessons to their children about marriage and morality. They teach an important truth about life: *Children do not grow up when they can take care of themselves; they really grow up when they can take care of others—and want to.*

It seems that the attitude of children toward each parent mirrors the attitude of the other parent. When a husband honors his wife, puts her first in family life, then the children follow his example; they honor and obey their mother. When a wife honors her husband in first place, the children grow to esteem him as a hero. The children see that, in Dad's eyes, Mom is a model for his daughters' future lives as outstanding women; and she is the kind of woman each son should someday marry. Similarly the children see, from Mom's example, that Dad is a model for each son's future life as a great man; and he is a pattern for the kind of man each daughter should someday choose as a husband.

Unified parents like this make the time to sit and talk about each child's growth in character—present needs and problems, steps that need to be taken and lessons taught, signs of progress, who shall handle what, and so on. Parents seem to find Sunday morning, even 20 minutes or a half-hour or so, as a good time for this sort of team discussion.

Unified parents do not let the children come between them, in anything. If a child poses a request to one parent (permission for a sleepover, for instance, or a new purchase, especially for some fad), each parent will hold off until he or she has first checked with the other: "Let me check with Dad first. . . .";"Let me talk with your mother, then I'll get back to you." This waiting to check is good for the children anyway; children who must wait for things learn to defer gratifications, which is a formative practice in itself. But more importantly, it teaches the children that each parent is determined to collaborate with the other in a unified leadership. *Children have only one mind and one conscience, and must have one clear set of directions coming from both parents together.*

Effective parents refrain from quarreling in front of the children, something deeply harmful to family life. The parents may disagree and even argue about issues openly, but never to the point of heated and hurtful exchange. Many parents have a policy and practice of signalling each other (pointing to a watch, for instance, or giving a "time out" sign) if one or the other senses that a disagreement is getting emotionally out of hand; this is a signal to drop the subject for now, put off discussion until later, when out of the children's sight. By then, of course, most of the heat has abated and peace can be restored.

Such parents, of course, absolutely never contradict each other about a disciplinary matter in front of the children. This seriously undercuts their authority, something to be avoided at all costs. Any disagreement must be worked out, mostly by compromise, in personal, private discussion.

Finally, successful parents are quick to apologize. A great family is one in which everyone, parents and children, sacrifices to put aside pride and express sincere regret for any offense given, even if unintended. "I'm sorry . . ." is one of the most powerful binding forces in family life. Christ said, "Blessed are the peacemakers," and he blesses every family that strives for peace.

Before moving on here, something needs to be said about single parents, those valiant men and women who must strive by themselves, without a spouse at home, to raise their children well. This is a great, heroic challenge, but many single parents manage to succeed.

How do they do this? Widows and widowers rely on the spiritual presence of their deceased spouse. The children are led to continue honoring him or her, and thus this loved one still abides in the family to influence the children's moral direction: "Your father (mother) would want you to act this way, and is watching over you from heaven. . . ."

Divorced and separated parents must take a different approach, but they too work toward confident and "unified" direction. They have several traits in common.

First, they struggle to forgive the missing spouse. They bear no personal ill will. The fighting has stopped, and there is peace in the heart. The Christian principle, "hate the sin, love the sinner," marks their attitude toward the one who has left. As much as possible, they lead the children to forgive and understand and never stop loving the missing one, no matter how much wrong has been done in the past.

Secondly, they refuse to see themselves as victims. They accept what has happened as a fact. They look to the future, not to the past, and they are determined that their children will grow up with sound conscience and character. They make an all-out effort to ensure that the flaws and mistakes of their marriage will not afflict the future marriages of their children.

Third, they put all their trust in God's fatherly care. They turn to God to help them to live as both father and mother to their children, relying on God to help them go beyond their limitations. In family life, God somehow takes the place of the missing spouse.

Control of the media

Successful parents rightly see the electronic media as *rivals* for their children's minds and hearts. They are determined to win in this rivalry.

The parents exercise discriminating control over what is watched on television and otherwise presented by films, music, and video games. They realize that these devices often—but not always—present the exact opposite of the virtues. In place of faith, hope, and charity, the media can portray a materialistic outlook on life. In place of sound judgment, they often foster mindless emotionalism, where wants become needs. Instead of responsibility, they promote vanity and self-centered disregard for the dignity and rights of others. In place of fortitude and temperance, they glamorize consumerist softness, escapism, and self-indulgence (including recreational sex) as normal life, admirable and worthy of young people's imitation.

At the same time, these parents know that there is much good in the media and that there is such a thing as healthy, moderate electronic recreation. The parents thus *use* the media in reasonable, intelligent ways that promote unified family life—ways that bring the family together.

They allow only one television in the house, so as to better manage it responsibly. Together, the family watches sports events, good films and high-quality shows, news programs, and documentaries. And that *is all they watch.*

The parents choose what is watched and when. Children can make requests and suggestions, of course, but the parents do the deciding. This leadership enhances the parents' authority, too. Since the electronic media are powerful forces in children's eyes, then parents who exercise this discriminating control appear *even more powerful* to the children, a valuable lesson in itself.

What the parents aim at here is not merely to protect the children but rather to teach lessons of discernment. Through the parents' judgment and exercise of rightful authority, the children learn to accept what is good, reject what is wrong, and know the difference.

There is a flat rule in the Christian family: We will have nothing in this home that glamorizes materialism and serves to undo our parental lessons of Christian life. This means no pornography (or anything like it), no gratuitous violence, no portrayals of disrespect for the rights and dignity of others.

This holds for television programs, movies, books, magazines, video games, music lyrics, and posters. We will not have
these offensive things in our house under any circumstances,
period.

Children growing up today need to learn this moral lesson and to learn it for life. After all, our present culture has
turned the age-old moral distinction (right from wrong) into
a question of *age*: "Under 17 not admitted . . . For mature au-
diences only . . . Adult entertainment," and the like. It's a small
wonder that children today think that after age sixteen, anything goes. They need to see their parents live by Christian
principles. We are all children of God and must love and obey
him all our lives. No matter what our age, we are obligated
to live in God's friendship. Christian morality binds adults as
well as children.

When the media are kept under discerning control this
way, some wonderful things happen in the family. Parents and
children find time to know and love each other thoroughly;
there is much more time in family life. Children grow strong
in body and mind through sports, chores, games, hobbies,
reading, and conversation. Children deepen in judgment, responsibility, perseverance, self-control. They collect memories of family life together that will last them a lifetime and
give strength to the families they will later form.

Lessons of integrity

Successful parents use the terms *integrity* and *honor* in
family life and teach the children what these mean.

The word "integrity" is related to the words "integer,"
"integrate," and "disintegrate." It means *unity* or *oneness*.

Integrity means unity of intention, word, and action—that we mean what we say, we say what we mean, and we keep our word.

Lies and broken promises have no part in our lives. We tell the truth and we keep our commitments, even if doing this involves personal sacrifice.

Nearly all children will sometimes spontaneously lie to avoid blame or responsibility. Lying and weeping are their principal defenses against adult power. Many successful parents handle the problem this way: When they suspect their child is lying (especially in a fairly important matter), they tell him or her the following—"Go into your room for five minutes and think things over, then come out and tell the truth *on your honor.* Whatever you say on your honor, I will believe. But it absolutely must be the truth, for there's a big difference between telling a lie and *being a liar.*"

Parents who resort to this position, putting their children on their honor, are almost never disappointed, especially if this family custom begins in young childhood. When the children tell the truth, the parents give a tiny punishment for the original wrongdoing but they lavish praise on the children for their integrity: a hug and kiss, and "I'm proud of you for telling the truth. . . ."

This custom is immensely important for children, especially later when they are adolescents. Nearly all teens will complain to parents, "Why don't you trust me?" Parents of teens must be able to answer sincerely, "We trust your integrity, and always have. We will always put faith in your honesty and good intentions. What we mistrust, for now, is your *judgment,* and only because of your present inexperience. Experience brings better judgment. When you have grown in experience, we will trust you entirely—in judgment as well as integrity."

Honor and integrity also pertain to promises, to commitments of every sort. So children must learn an important lesson: We do not make promises lightly . . . but if we make them, we must keep them. Please note the "we" here; parents should not make promises lightly to their children, either. This includes threats. Parents should never threaten a punishment that they are unprepared to carry out.

All this teaching about integrity and honor is vitally important for the children's future. To lie or break promises is offensive to God. A habit of lying, moreover, can harm or destroy children's future careers. Liars get fired.

And, of course, the clear notion of keeping our promises—putting our sacred honor behind every serious commitment—is direct preparation for a holy and permanent marriage.

"Affectionate assertiveness"

In the area of corrective discipline—leading the children to or making them do what is right—effective Christian parents seem to practice what may be called "affectionate assertiveness." That is, they confidently assert what the children need to do, and they do this with affection. Even when they feel they must punish the children (administering "memorable correction," as noted before), this is done with a spirit of love. The deep and underlying affection may be eclipsed briefly by strong words and righteous parental anger, but love is always there and affection quickly reasserts itself.

To look at the matter another way, Christian parents correct the fault, not the person. They "hate the sin, but love the sinner." They love their children too much to let them grow up with faults uncorrected.

Such parents see "no" as a loving word. They know that their children must hear this word from time to time when appropriate, or they will never be able to say "no" to themselves. Children who never experience loving parental denial cannot form the habit of self-denial, and this could lead to disaster.

How many young people's problems and tragedies in life—substance abuse, auto accidents and fatalities, promiscuity and its consequences, aimless careers, broken marriages—arise from a lack of affectionate parental direction in childhood, including absence of the word "no"? Effective Christian parents never forget this. It gives them the strength to persevere.

Indeed it seems that *why* parents punish is more important than *how*.

Some parents have no problem with spanking youngsters when they deem this necessary, especially if the children are too young to grasp the meaning of words. Other parents are temperamentally loath to administer corporal punishment; they prefer "time out" or grounding or some other unpleasant consequence for misbehavior. Who is right here?

It would seem that the parents' motives and their self-confidence are what count, not the particular choice of punishment. If a parent's punishment comes from love for the child, for his or her long-term welfare, then it is effective no matter what form it takes. Children sense this somehow, mysteriously: My parents correct me because they love me. Deep down they know this, especially if the parent is quick to forgive affectionately once the wrong is undone and apologies are made.

Parental *confidence* is also important. In all of life, authority must be proportional to responsibility, and this holds true for parents as well.

Parents have an enormous responsibility for their children, especially to God. So they must have, and must exercise, rightful authority. One of the definitions of authority is "the right to be obeyed." Parents have every right to be obeyed by their children, and effective parents know it.

So, although effective parents may be unconfident about many things, they have every confidence in their authority. They may doubt what is the right decision in a touchy family situation, but they have no doubt of their right to make a decision in the first place—and to make it stick. They do not let indecision lead to harmful inaction, for they know that neglect in important matters is the greatest mistake of all.

But which matters are important and which are not? Here are some helpful guidelines from the experience of other parents:

It is important to remember that all smaller children misbehave from time to time. This is a fact, unavoidable and completely natural.

They thoughtlessly track mud in the house, leave toys and clothes strewn about, honestly forget to do chores, and the like. This is kiddish neglect and forgetful misbehavior. You should correct these, of course, but not necessarily all the time, every time, lest you nearly lose your mind. Some of these problems they will outgrow, and others will be corrected over time—especially if you concentrate your corrective efforts on more important concerns.

One of the more important matters is misbehavior that involves infringement of other people's rights, especially siblings. When your children infringe on the rights of siblings or friends—for instance, name-calling, hitting, taking possessions without permission, rummaging through others' belongings—they should be corrected strongly every time. Children must learn, especially after age five, to live justly and charitably with others. They must grow to grasp that other people have rights and feelings, and we are obligated to restrain our selfish impulses and respect these people's rights.

In a sense, your efforts to enforce justice and charity among the children is a direct, long-term preparation for the way they will later treat their spouses. Their behavior at home now is an apprenticeship for their later marriages. Look around you: adults who still treat their grown-up siblings with indifference or hostility tend to have serious marital problems as well, and their own children are often out of control.

When Our Lord said, "Blessed are the peacemakers . . .," he was also referring to parents of small children. Parents who persevere in making peace between brothers and sisters, teaching lessons of moral responsibility among them, see their efforts pay off later—when their grown-up children show lifelong affectionate regard for each other.

This leaves the most important matters, those areas where the children must be corrected vigorously every single time. Misbehavior in these areas can seriously damage the children, now and later, and must never go uncorrected. There are three:

First, when the children *show disrespect for you personally*— when they strike you (or strike you back) or direct abusive language to you.

Secondly, when they *show disrespect for your authority*— saying "no" back to you, or flatly refusing to obey you, or purposely neglecting to do what you have directed.

Third, when they *tell a deliberate lie,* especially when put on their honor.

These three types of misbehavior are so important that you must come down with full force against them, giving a "memorable correction" that will not be forgotten.

Why is this? Because everything else you have to teach the children, all your other lessons of right and wrong, depend utterly on their respect for you, for your rightful authority, and for their own word of honor. If you surrender here, you lose everything. You lose your children. But if you succeed with these matters, you can lead them effectively in everything else.

To use a rough analogy: In our criminal justice system, it is possible to negotiate a plea bargain and reduced sentence for most crimes. In two areas, however, there is no negotiation and the full force of the law comes down hard. Those areas are contempt of court and perjury. Anyone who defies the court's authority or who lies under oath can expect the severest penalties every time. The reason is obvious: without respect for the court and for telling the truth under oath, our entire justice system would collapse; the courts might as well shut down. In the courts as in the family, people must respect rightful authority and honor-given word.

If you concentrate your correction in these areas—authority, justice, and truth—you will have relatively few problems with your children in the other, lesser matters, especially as they grow older.

Parents who display confident moral leadership to their children are the ones who eventually succeed. This moral leadership implies, of course, that you give children good example in the responsible exercise of your authority. You adhere to standards of justice and truth in your dealings with them. This means, among other things, that you respect your children's rights.

Yes, your children do have rights, not because they are children, but because they are people—and all people have rights. When your children sense your earnest determination to be *fair* with them, they will come to respect your rightful authority.

When it comes to matters of discipline and punishment, then, what are the rights of your children that you should respect? They are the same rights we adults expect in our dealings with one another:

- The right to know what is expected of us: Rules should be spelled out clearly beforehand, along with the consequences for non-compliance. Arbitrary and capricious order-giving to people (of any age) provokes their frustration and rebellion. We all resent being punished because we could not read someone's mind. (See next chapter for list of rules.)

- The right to presumption of innocence: Unless a parent has personally witnessed a child's misconduct, he or she should suspend judgment until the child has had a chance to explain. Appearances are sometimes deceiving. Justice depends on facts, not hastily formed "impressions."

- The right to proportionate punishment: Heavy punishment for minor infractions is inherently unjust. Because overreaction nearly always stems from anger, parents should wait until they have calmed down before allotting punishment: "We'll settle this later. . . ." Another tack is to let the child propose a suitable way of making amends; remarkably, what a child suggests in these circumstances is usually reasonable and fair.

- The right to just apology: If a parent has made a mistake (in judgment or excessive punishment), he or she owes an apology. Children will overlook and forgive occasional injustice if they see their parents' consistent determination to be fair.

- The right to a fresh start: Once amends are made, the matter is dropped, period. Dredging up past faults that had been allegedly forgiven and forgotten is poisonous to family life. (This pertains as well to husband and wife in their dealings with each other.)

One final matter here should give you greater hope and confidence. Parents who try overmuch to *control* their children, who are preoccupied with control for its own sake, meet with frustration and discouragement; but parents who seek to *form* their children, to lead them toward responsible Christian adulthood, find peace and satisfaction.

In the long run, it seems, their mistakes along the way do not really matter. A determined long-term strategy, even with occasional tactical mistakes, is what triumphs in the end.

In summary, Christian parents treat their children the way God treats all of us: with unqualified affectionate love, clear standards of right and wrong, high expectations, respect for responsible freedom, just correction of faults, and readiness to forgive.

Your vocational work to form your children this way, as God's chosen instrument for their earthly and eternal happiness, is a great apostolate. And that great apostle St. Paul said words that apply to you as a Christian parent: "We know that all things work for good for those who love God, who are called according to his purpose" (Romans 8: 28).

When you turn to God for his help in your family life, you can be confident he will never leave your prayers unanswered.

4

Standards and Rules

A S WE HAVE SEEN SO FAR, a successful Christian family has a clear sense of mission and confident parental leadership. This brings us to the third element, a binding structure—a clear set of high standards for attitudes and deportment in the home—that is, a set of rules.

Children need to know what is expected of them. In fact, we all do.

When children grow up in a family governed by high personal standards and clear, manifestly fair rules, they grow in confidence. Knowing that their parents are in control of things, they feel safe, secure, and loved. A loving, secure environment leads children to have confidence in their parents, and this in turn builds their self-confidence. The children's powers are directed toward solving problems and deflected away from creating problems. This acquired habit of solving problems successfully leads to self-confidence. Finally, children learn through practice to control their impulses, to grow in self-mastery. Children who can master themselves are prepared to master the direction of their lives.

Clear and reasonable rules show children where the lines exist between right and wrong, those borderlines where our actions and neglects begin to infringe on the rights of others—God, parents, siblings, and other people in our lives. The rules say, in effect, "Within these limiting lines, we are free; but beyond them, we offend . . . and we must not offend." Constantly, every day in countless ways, the rules teach the children sound moral judgment, a sense of responsibility, and self-control.

In other words, the rules give ongoing practice in the virtues.

As said before, parents teach mostly by example, not just directives. Consequently, the rules in any successful family begin with the word "we." That is, the standards bind the parents as well as the children. The father and mother live by these standards, and they insist that the children do the same. In essence, what the parents do is show the children how we Christian adults live responsibly, and then they lead or make the children follow suit. Thus the parents make no demands on the children that they fail to live by themselves; their children can never justly accuse them of hypocrisy.

Experience shows that rules like this—clear, reasonable, and binding everyone in the family—have a way of passing down through generations. When the children later form families of their own, they remember the way their parents led them, and they adopt the same standards for their own families. In this way, they do what God commands all of us: they honor their father and mother. The finest way we honor our parents is to adopt their principles and religious convictions, internalize and live by them all our lives, and pass them on to our own children whole and intact.

Here are the rules that, in some form or another, seem to characterize the most successful Christian families. . . .

1. *We respect the rights and feelings of everyone.*

- We do not engage in name-calling or put-downs.
- We do not use foul language or profanity.
- We say to everyone: *please, thank you, I'm sorry, I give my word.* . . .
- We do not interrupt; we wait to talk. (No interrupting parents when they're talking with others, either personally or on the phone—and then we say, "Excuse me, please. . . .")
- We do not talk back when corrected.
- We do not make promises lightly; but if we do, we keep our word.
- We treat appointments and deadlines as binding promises; if we cannot keep them, despite our best efforts, we render sincere apology.
- We respect each other's privacy and personal property; we knock before entering a closed room, get prior permission before borrowing.
- We do not bicker or quarrel at the dinner table.
- We do not gossip about people or otherwise talk negatively about people behind their backs.
- We mind our own business; we stay out of matters that do not concern us.
- We greet adults with good manners and a firm handshake.
- We give guests the best of what we have.

- We practice good telephone manners.

- If we have offended, we apologize—even if we did not mean to give offense. We put justice and charity ahead of our pride.

- If someone renders an apology to us, we accept it—for it is dishonorable to refuse to make peace.

2. *We all contribute to make our home an attractive, civilized, and efficiently run place to live.*

- We enter the house with clean footwear only; if we accidentally make a mess, we clean it up.

- Males do not wear hats or caps indoors.

- We do not return a car home with less than a quarter-tank of gas.

- We do not slam doors; if we do so by accident, we say, "I'm sorry. . . ."

- We do not bring "outdoor activities" indoors: running, ball-playing, missile-throwing, roughhouse wrestling, unreasonable shouting.

- We do not shout messages from one room to another; we walk to wherever someone is and then deliver the message in normal voice.

- We do not consume food or drink in bedrooms. No eating outside the kitchen, dining room, and recreation room.

- We do not overindulge in food or drink; no unauthorized eating between meals.

- We hang up clothing when not in use; all clothing is

in one of three places—on us, in closets and dressers, or in the laundry for cleaning.

- We lay out clothes at night for the next morning.
- If old enough to do so, we make our own beds in the morning.
- We put playthings and tools away when not in use.
- If we've eaten off, or drunk out of, something—then we rinse or wash it and put it where it belongs.
- If we've borrowed something, we return it where it belongs; if we have lost a borrowed item, we either replace it or pay for it.
- We fulfill our "house responsibilities" (our chores) promptly and to the best of our ability. This includes assignments for school.
- We can all make suggestions ("input") about many things in family life, but parents make decisions in serious matters.
- We do not aim for "results" but rather for *personal best effort*.

3. We give people the information they need to carry out their responsibilities.

- When we go out, we always inform: *Where? With whom? When will we return?*
- If we are going to be late, we call.
- We get prior permission, with at least one day's notice, for sleepovers, camping trips, and the like. Insufficient notice may mean no permission.

- We come straight home from school, except with prior permission.

- We bring home all new friends and introduce them to our parents.

- We return from social events at a reasonable hour, one that has been previously agreed upon.

- We take phone messages intelligently: name of caller, time called, phone number of caller (if applicable), gist of message (if any), name or initials of person who took call.

- In general, we avoid "unpleasant surprises" in the family.

4. *We use the media to promote family life and welfare; we do not permit media to work against family life and welfare.*

- We have nothing in the home that offends our moral principles or that treats people like mere objects (materialism): this means no pornography, no gratuitous violence, no depictions of rudeness or gross vulgarity. This pertains to TV, movies, video games, music lyrics, posters.

- We will watch TV and video movies together: sports, high-quality films and programs, news and documentaries . . . and that's it.

- We do not watch TV on school nights . . . unless we watch something together as noted above.

- If we squabble over TV or video games, we get one warning to stop; if problems persist, the activity is terminated.

- We keep use of the telephone under reasonable control: no calls during dinner or homework or after 10:00 P.M.; no outgoing calls after 9:30 P.M. except for emergencies; calls limited to 15 minutes.

- We devote most of family life to healthy work and play, not glued to the tube. We spend our time in conversation, reading, study, chores, and games—getting to know and appreciate each other in the few precious years we have together as a family.

5. We love and serve God above all things; we thank him and ask his help for our needs and those of others.

- We thank God by worshipping him together on Sunday.

- We dress well for church—because God is more important than anyone, and we give him our very best.

- We pray before meals and bedtime and on other special occasions. God lives in our family, not just in church.

- We treat clergy with respect, gratitude, and affection . . . and we pray for them and their needs.

- We pray for each other, for the Church, and for all those in need. We rely on God's help to forgive our sins and lead us to surpass our limitations.

- We are always conscious that God is watching over us with his fatherly protection . . . and our lives thus become a sporting adventure.

There are many variations on these rules, of course, and the list here is by no means exhaustive. Perhaps you would add to these, or delete some. This is unimportant. What really counts is that *some* standards bind the family together and build strengths within the hearts and minds of the children.

Bear in mind, too, that living by these standards every day is a formidable challenge for any parent. You need a great passionate ideal to persevere, especially if you feel yourself flagging or you grow discouraged from children's apparent lack of progress. That passionate ideal is, of course, your love for each of them. Take courage and do not give up, just as God never gives up on you and never will.

Remember the promise God has made to parents who love and serve him, spoken through the prophet Isaiah (59: 21): "My spirit which is upon you, and my words that I have put into your mouth, shall never leave your mouth, nor the mouths of your children, nor the mouths of your children's children, from now on and forever, says the Lord."

Have faith that, with his help and your own patient perseverance, you will one day see your children living by these standards on their own, as a lifelong habit, even before they are out of their teens, but especially when they start their own families—or when they serve and strengthen other families through apostolic celibacy. The joy you have at that time, the sheer delight of victory, will be part of God's "hundred-fold" reward to you, his good and faithful servant.

★ ★ ★

Thus far in this book, we have seen the larger strategic vision of effective Christian parenthood: how mission, leadership, and formative family structure all work together to raise children into great men and women. The rest of these chapters look more closely at how parents work on tactical details of children's upbringing.

What will follow here is a more specific understanding of the basic (cardinal) virtues—judgment, responsibility, courageous perseverance, self-mastery—and the supernatural virtues of faith, hope, and charity.

Since charity, love for God and others, is the greatest virtue (see I Corinthians 13: 1-13), we shall elaborate on how parents teach children to love and serve God throughout their lives with all their heart, soul, mind, and strength.

5

Sound Judgment and Conscience

Sound judgment and conscience form the basis for the other virtues.

Throughout the course of their lives, your children cannot purposely *do* what is right unless they *know* what is right. They cannot be expected to act justly if they do not know what is just. They cannot practice their faith if they remain uninstructed in it. They cannot truly love God and serve him sacrificially unless they first know him. They cannot assess events and people (say, a prospective spouse) without some rational criteria for doing so. They cannot direct their own lives without solid, compelling reasons for choosing one way rather than another.

To be sure, children also need will-power, heart, and personal toughness in order to live rightly. Right knowledge alone, without these other strengths, is insufficient; it becomes an inert bundle of good intentions. In short, judgment and conscience provide direction for life's important choices, and the other virtues transform those choices into action. *Good judgment leads to good choices, and good choices lead to a good life.*

Though children sometimes display dazzling flashes of insight to truth, they do not enter this world with strengths

of judgment. Without teaching and directed practice in
moral discernment, children grow into adolescence with
the flaws of childish thinking largely intact. Their choice-
making remains powerfully influenced by emotions,
appetites, peer pressures, and vanity. Their conscience
remains a shapeless mass of feelings blown about by circumstances and rationalized self-interest. They are easy
prey for propaganda, and they are often paralyzed by indecision.

What we are really speaking about here is that elusive
and transcendental power called *wisdom*, without which life
becomes a directionless experience of sense impressions.
Your children need to learn wisdom from you. They need
to acquire your own powers of discerning assessment, your
principles and convictions about truth and justice.

Since this power of discernment embraces so much of
life, it is difficult to define exactly. Nonetheless, it is real; we
know it when we see it in people. How may we describe it?
Here are some approaches. . . .

Sound judgment is the ability to recognize the good, the
true, and the beautiful when we see these things—and to distinguish them from the evil, the false, and the sordid. It is the
power to make *distinctions*.

It is the ability to understand human nature and life-
experience: to grasp people's motivations, values, and priorities in life. In one word, it is *shrewdness*.

It is the acquired habit of considering present circumstances in light of *past causes* and *future implications*—historical origins and future trends. It is the habit of asking "Why?"
and "What if. . . ?" and "Where are we headed?"

Related to this, it is the habit of reflecting on likely future consequences for present free decisions, especially consequences that affect the lives of others. Simply put, it is to think ahead.

It is respect for learning and intellectual accomplishment—in a word, *culture*.

In the area of morality (the interplay of rights and obligations), it is *conscience*. It is the habit of asking, in situations of moral choice, "How does this square with what God has commanded me through the Church and my parents and teachers? What must I do here to please God?"

In sum, it is *to use one's mind like a responsible, competent, morally upright adult.*

This is where you, as a parent, come in. Your task is to teach your children to think as you do: that is, to adopt your principled convictions as the basis for their discernment of right and wrong and their whole outlook on life. As the definitions above suggest, you need to form them in habits of reflecting, asking questions, deliberating, learning from experience.

All this, in turn, implies frequent conversation in family life. You need to make time to talk with your children and listen to them carefully, helping them to understand, leading them to follow your own judgment.

As you set about this teaching, please bear several important matters in mind. . . .

First, in this virtue as in the others, you teach mainly by example, and often when you are least aware of it. Children have selective hearing, as you are well aware, but they miss little of what they see. In countless details of family life, they can see your discerning judgment in action: your choice of books and magazines, TV programs, movies, friends, heroes, manners, rules for the home—choices that convey your judgment in action. What remains is to *explain why.*

Moreover, children learn an enormous amount from what they *overhear* at home. When they overhear your conversations with others—your spouse, other siblings, friends and invited guests, even "arguments" with the television—they are absorbing snatches of your judgment, fitting all this together with what you tell them directly.

Naturally, children overhear much more at home, and witness more around them, when their attention is not diverted by television. When children sit before the tube in a trance-like stare, they miss out on their parents' conversational interactions. What they do not hear, they do not learn.

Secondly, and related to the last point, when you get the television under control, you find much more time in family life for conversation.

Time at dinner is extended, with no one in a hurry to go anywhere, and the dinner becomes a more leisurely conversational get-together. Time spent together in washing dishes, playing board games, answering questions about homework, driving together in a car, doing chores—all these occasions make for conversation, mulling questions, thinking things through together. Children learn, a little bit at a time, about their parents' reasoning and judgment. When parents want this to happen, they somehow make the occasions for it and take advantage of occasions that happen along. When your *why* is strong enough, you can find the *how.*

Third, you must respect your children's freedom of thought. You must clearly distinguish moral judgments from matters of free opinion and taste. Your intention is that your children, all their lives, will live by moral principles that bind all of us, whatever our age; and so you insist that they respect your authority, respect others' rights, and join you in worshipping God. But as they grow older, and especially through their teens, they are free to disagree with you in matters of opinion and taste—and you respect that freedom.

In other words, you distinguish between morals and *mores*. You put your foot down on matters that threaten their souls, that offend God and infringe on others' rights. And you have a right to direct deportment in matters of manners, choice of school and friends, family life, and family honor. (For instance, they may not dress in such a way as to embarrass the family.) But you make no dogmas out of clearly opinionable matters: choice of political party or candidate, taste in music, recreational preferences, eventual choice of career, and the like. You may hope your sons and daughters will follow your example in these matters, but you may not rightly insist upon it. There is such a thing as being too "principled."

When you act this way, leading your children toward responsible use of their freedom, they will know which of your convictions are really matters of moral principle and which are not. The moral matters thus stand out in importance, as they should. Your children will not be tempted, as many teens and young adults are, to rebel and reject all their parents' "dogmas," the God-given ones as well as the contrived. Indeed, young adults raised by parents who steadily respect their rightful freedoms, who teach them and trust them to think for themselves, are the ones most inclined to emulate their parents in nearly everything.

Finally, strive yourself to continue growing in judgment. Apply your mind as much as possible to reading, study, and conversation with people whose judgment you respect. We continue learning all our lives, but especially if we set our minds to it. When you have doubts about a correct course of action (as perhaps in the above section, distinguishing morals from opinionable matters), talk the issue out with people of sound judgment; this, of course, includes your spouse. Regularly consulting a spiritual director is one excellent way to do this.

In this area, too, you give your children good example. They will see you have an open mind, a respect for learning, a willingness to learn from others. If you read a lot, your children will likely pick up reading as a habit. If you can read some of the better books they are reading in school, you can exchange thoughts and questions with your children, leading them to draw out lessons about people and life. In any event, whatever you do to continue developing your judgment teaches your children some important lessons:

- Learning is a lifetime pursuit; the years in school are just a beginning.
- The most important lessons about life are learned outside of school.
- People who enjoy learning retain a youthful outlook all their lives.

Reading and culture

Blessed Josemaria Escriva, the founder of Opus Dei, once said, "These world crises are crises of saints. . . ." (*The Way*, # 301).

By the time your children are in their late teens, they should know what the term "saints" means. But they should also know the meaning of "world crises." They cannot do this if they remain ignorant about human affairs, those significant events in political and social life that affect them and their future families. At some point, their vision of the world needs to extend beyond the narrow childhood boundaries of family, school, sports, and neighborhood fast-food restaurants.

They cannot become leaders unless they understand people, all kinds of people. They cannot elect principled public officials unless they know what good or harm political officials can do. They cannot influence social developments later if they fail to understand the problems of our time.

In short, your children need to be led out of the naive social and historical provincialism that characterizes so many young people today. History teaches us that peace and prosperity are not states of nature, that wars and economic depressions come and go, and they may come again in your children's lifetimes. Adults of every generation, including your children's, must face massive social problems and cope with them as best they can.

Do your older children and teenagers understand these realities?

Are you preparing them to become informed, responsible citizens as well as parents? Do they know what is going on in the world, good and bad, and how "world crises" arise from ignorance and evil in the human heart?

For centuries, reading and conversation were the ways by which children learned about the world outside the family. Take your cue from this. You should lead your children to read, and to read with judgment and discrimination.

Start with newspapers. By the time your children are entering high school, they should read something in the newspaper besides the sports and comics. The paper's news and editorial sections show events and trends (imperfectly to be sure) that could someday affect your children's lives: their employment, the moral fabric of their society, the physical and moral safety of their families. By your example and conversation, by reading along with them, you can lead them to understand. In a sense, you prepare them to protect themselves and their families.

Great parents protect their children best this way—by preparing them to protect themselves and the others in their lives.

Your children should read other works as well, as many as possible, even light fiction. If your children develop a habit of reading, then later, when they are led to read great literary works, they will recognize why these are great. Literary masterpieces will stand out from the children's previous reading. Great literature and history and biography teach us about people, about the triumphs and follies of our fellow humans. This is why they are collectively called the "humanities."

Children can learn about heroes and heroism in their reading. They can see, through examples, how ordinary people meet great challenges and overcome them. They can meet literary characters and historical figures who embody the virtues: judgment, responsibility, personal courage, and self-control. They can see how the saints lived these virtues heroically, and how their lives achieved greatness through faith, hope, and the love for God and souls. A virtuous life is one of adventure, and the saints' adventurous lives inspire us all: no one enjoys life more than a saint, and anyone can become one.

Please remember this: Your children need heroes. Young people are always searching for a life to imitate. If they do not have heroes, then they follow after "celebrities" and clowns.

A virtuous life set before them teaches more than any set of rules for conduct; in fact, it gives depth and meaning to such rules. When children have heroes, they eventually come to see the heroism of their parents. Later in life, as they start their own families, they look back on Mom and Dad as great people.

In a Christian home, then, reading is much more than a pleasant pastime. It is a preparation for life.

Distinctions

One way to understand the virtue of sound judgment is to see it as the acquired power to make distinctions.

We see this even in our word usage. The word "clever" is related to "cleave" and "cleaver"—cutting through something and separating it into parts, especially opposites. A "sharp" mind also enjoys this power to cut and separate. And to "deliberate" means literally to weigh things as on a balance scale, to evaluate the pro's and con's of something, especially a projected course of action.

The overall task of parents is to lead children out of their inborn fuzziness of thinking, their strong tendency to judge matters emotionally, indiscriminately, and skewed by self-interest. A glance through the works of the great teachers— Socrates, Plato, Aristotle, Aquinas—shows their constant emphasis on making distinctions. They taught their disciples to discern. You, as a parent-teacher, have the same challenge with your own "disciples" at home.

Your task is complicated by our present society's *ethos* of blurring distinctions, covering over or eliminating differences in matters of morals and even common-sense understanding—right and wrong, truth and opinion, objective and subjective, conscience and "feelings," even male and female. For this reason, you need to work conscientiously to build your children's powers of ethical and intellectual discernment.

So, what are the distinctions you need to teach your children as they grow up? What should they be able to discern by the time they reach adulthood? Here are some examples. No doubt you and your spouse could add others. . . .

- compassionate understanding, from hostility or indifference
- enjoyment in moderation, from self-indulgent excess
- real heroes, from entertainers and "celebrities"
- clear and strong conscience, from self-interested "feelings"
- rights, from interests
- a true friend, from an acquaintance or accomplice
- calculated risk-taking, from impulsiveness
- good manners, from boorishness

- "class," from vulgarity
- healthy self-respect, from arrogant pride
- assertiveness, from aggressiveness
- integrity, from pragmatic disregard for truth and keeping one's word
- honorable competition and sportsmanship, from ruthless ambition ("win at any cost")
- patience, from impetuousness
- reasoned opinions, from "feelings" and "impressions"
- love, from eroticism
- healthy skepticism and shrewdness, from cynicism
- God's law (moral rights), from man-made law (legal rights)
- ethical public service, from ideological politics
- humor and healthy wit, from mean-spirited ridicule
- courageous perseverance, from escapism
- normal and inevitable difficulties, from "hassles"
- mature order and neatness, from childish messiness
- professionalism, from carelessness and amateurish sloppiness
- proven fact, from assumption
- presumption of innocence, from rash judgment
- healthy effort, from sloth
- love for the sinner, from hatred of sin
- minding one's own business, from gossip and meddling
- apology and forgiveness, from spiteful grudge-bearing

- responsible spirit of service, from childish self-centeredness
- Christian life-outlook, from materialism

As mentioned above, this list is by no means complete. You and your spouse may add to it as you see fit. (In fact, this would be a helpful and enlightening exercise.) The main point here is to see the sort of strength you are trying to build in your children's judgment. You work constantly to help your children distinguish right from wrong, good from evil, the noble from the sordid.

Moreover, you work to inculcate a *vocabulary* for these concepts.

Your children should hear and understand the important words that name aspects of right living—integrity, honor, conscience, justice, apology, charity, and the rest—as well as their opposites named above.

Reasoned explanations

In the last chapter, you could see how the list of rules for the home contained implicitly an ongoing practice of the virtues. Carrying out these rules consistently, day after day, teaches the children responsibility, self-control, perseverance, and the supernatural strengths of faith, hope, and charity.

From time to time, of course, the children will question these rules, either by challenge or by honest inquiry. Your answers to their questions, your explaining the reasons behind the rules, teaches the children sound judgment and conscience. For instance. . . .

Why can't we argue at the dinner table? Answer: We can discuss and disagree about many things at dinner, but not to the point of heated bickering and quarreling. Dinner is a sacred time for us; it is one of the few occasions when we gather in family unity, and we ask God to bless it with our prayers before meals. Quarreling should be avoided at all other times, of course, but we flatly insist it will not be tolerated when we dine. Besides, it is good for all of us to practice complete self-restraint at least once or twice a day, as a way of building it into a permanent strength. Finally, family harmony is especially important to your mother, and she deserves to achieve it at least once a day during dinner—as a victory and a reward.

Why do we have to put things back where they belong? Because doing this teaches consideration for the rights and needs of others. Sloppiness is self-centered; order is other-centered. We cannot serve other people effectively unless we have a habit of considering their needs.

A sound marriage builds on this habit: putting other people's needs ahead of our comfort and convenience. Each child does this now for parents and siblings, and will do it later (we hope) for spouse and children—as well as friends, bosses, clients, customers, and anyone else who needs help.

Why can't we bring "outdoors activities" indoors? Because the home is a place where we learn to practice civilized restraint, to control our impulses for the sake of harmony. Out-of-control impulses can cause physical damage to property and cause grief to your mother; so we must exercise self-control when we enter the house. Later in life, uncontrolled impulses can cause even greater damage to ourselves and others. So we must get control over ourselves, and this rule is one way to build the habit.

Why can't we watch what everyone else watches on TV? Because immoral programs offend God, and we do not do this. Pleasing God and avoiding sin is always more important than conformity and public opinion.

People who live by Christian principles are always slightly "different," and there is nothing wrong with this. As for those programs that are morally blameless but a waste of time, we would rather see you grow stronger in mind and body through reading, games, and sports. Too much TV-watching is like chewing bubble gum: pleasant but essentially useless.

Why do we have to tell you where we're going, and why should we call if we're going to be late? Because we love you enough to worry about you. Parents today have enough to worry about in their children's lives; it is unfair and hurtful to cause your parents unnecessary worry.

Why do we always have to say please *and* thank you *and* I'm sorry? Because everyone has dignity, rights, and feelings; and good manners are our way of acknowledging this fact, internalizing a respect for others.

Why do we have to attend Mass on Sunday? Because God has commanded it, and we always obey him. He is our Father. We owe him worship and thanks and sacrificial love. We do not attend Mass for entertainment or social interchange; we do it because we want to *return* to him, to *give back* to him, a portion of his infinite love for each of us. The Mass is the perfect prayer for this because it was instituted by Christ himself.

And so on. . . .

Your children may not grasp your reasons for the rules, at least for now. You must persevere nonetheless, confident that someday they will.

And if your explanations take place while you are correcting their misdeeds, they may not like what they are hearing and emotionally resist it. No surprise. After all, no one likes being corrected, and you can pretty much ignore their moaning and groaning. If you sense they are persistently asking "Why?" just for an argument, you can just drop the subject: "I've already explained why, . . . so the matter is closed, period." Later, when emotions have cooled, the lessons will sink in. Despite appearances, the youngsters really are listening.

Looking back and ahead

Everyone likes stories, and children like them most of all. You and your spouse should go out of your way to tell stories centered on family history. This is especially important in our era, where ties to the extended family are weak and frayed.

The idea here is to give each of your children the notion that they are part of an ongoing family story. They had grandparents and forebears who were once their age, who moved from place to place, who served people with their jobs, who fell in love and married, who persevered in faith through wars and tough economic times—who were, in short, quietly heroic people. In a real sense, we are all descended from heroes.

You and your spouse should tell them about your own personal histories: your lives as children and teens, your ambitions and mistakes and hilarious blunders, your finding each other and your courtship, the great joy you had with the birth of each child, your ambitions and concerns for the future, your confidence in each of your children—that they carry this family adventure forward, living life to its fullest in the state of grace, preserving their family's faith and values intact and handing these on to their own children.

Bear something in mind: One sign of a healthy family is that the children know their parents well, and thus respect them. Children know what hobbies their father had as a child, what mischief he got punished for, how each parent used to celebrate Christmas, how each parent came to appreciate their parents as wonderful people, what Mom thought of Dad when she first met him, how they chose the name for each child, and so on. The children thus grow to know their parents inside out. Personal history—indeed any great story—implicitly teaches lessons about virtue and life. In subtle ways, children come to understand their parents' principles, why they think and act the way they do.

A parenthesis here, something for you to consider: Surely, now that you are a parent yourself, and especially as you reflect on your own childhood, you understand your parents' sacrifices and lessons as never before. So, if your parents are still alive, and if you have not really done so already, you should express your loving thanks to them from the bottom of your heart. You will make them very happy, and in a sense you will round out their lives in final victory. If they are already deceased, you can add to their happiness in heaven with your prayers of thanks to them. Gratitude is one of the most exquisite forms of love. In either case, expressing heartfelt thanks to your parents will please God, and it will strengthen the way you raise your children.

Life-lessons

One of the main jobs of parents is to teach their children those key lessons of life that are collectively called "wisdom." These are the lessons (generalizations, if you will) about life's experience that responsible, reflective adults recognize as true and important. They are basic understandings about human affairs and right living that pass from one generation to another.

They are lessons that young people learn mainly at home, not in school—though indeed many of them form moral themes in great literature. If we consider each human life (whether real or depicted in fiction) as an ongoing story, with chapters of experience along the way, then these life-lessons form the "moral" of the story: what we learn about life as we grow up.

There are scores of such life-lessons, and we recognize them as true when we see them. (Many form the themes of this book.) We may have heard them from parents when we were small, but failed to understand their true meaning until we finally grew up. In a real sense, we do not grow up until we finally understand the truth, the great wisdom, of our parents' lessons—"Mom and Dad were right. . . ."

Here are some such life-lessons:

- For those who love God, life becomes a grand and comic adventure.

- The real riches in life are strong faith, a clean conscience, the love of family and friends. Everything else is "extra."

- The happiest people are those who can forget their self-interests and direct their powers toward the welfare of others.

- If we seek happiness directly in life, it eludes us; we only grasp it when we try to give it to others.

- Marriage is not a business deal, a 50-50 proposition; it only works when each partner gives generously, abundantly, with little regard for return.

- A life given to sense pleasure is relentlessly greedy, never satisfied, ultimately lonely; but a life devoted to spirit—turned to God, goodness, truth, beauty—brings happiness and peace of mind.

- Time is a resource, scarce and irreplaceable; if we do not use it, we throw it away.

- Character is what we admire in people aside from their talents and despite their shortcomings.

- Responsibility is unavoidable, for we all answer to somebody: family, bosses, clients, customers, the law. Everybody answers to God.

- There's no such thing as a free lunch; every worthwhile achievement requires sacrificial effort.

- Deadlines are valuable, for there is such a thing as good stress; we do our best work when under reasonable pressure.

- Good friendship brings out the best in us.

- Respect is more important than popularity; if we have healthy self-respect, we win the respect of others.

- We can tell a lot about people by knowing their heroes, the people they most admire.

- It often requires more wisdom to take good advice than to give it.

- Nobody respects or trusts a liar, a gossip, a cynic, or a whiner.

- Any boss will tell you: In professional life, character and integrity count more for success than talent, skills, or credentials.

- Shallow blabbermouths seldom make it to the top in business; the real leaders are intelligent talkers and thoughtful listeners.

- When good-willed people are angry with each other, the cause is almost always some sort of misunderstanding.

- We do not really forgive unless we also entirely forget; to dwell on past grievances is evil and destructive.

- To refuse someone's sincere apology is grievously dishonorable.

- God put us on earth to serve him by serving others; we are born to serve, not to shop.

- People "in touch with their feelings" seldom amount to much; real achievement nearly always requires *overcoming* our feelings.

- Contending with occasional hardship is normal in life, and inevitable; anyone who cannot accept this reality turns into a bellyacher and a bore.

- There's no such thing as an ideal job. Every line of work, even one we like, has some aspect we find distasteful—paperwork, time pressures, commuting, erratic demands, and the like. Responsible people just accept this fact without complaint and get on with the job.

- Money is an instrument for the welfare of our loved ones and those in need—and that's all it is.

- Immature people do not distinguish between wants and needs.

- Nothing, absolutely nothing, is worth losing our soul.

- When we pray to God for his help, for a miracle, we start noticing coincidences.

- The secret for success in any part of life is to be moved by some great, passionate love.

- If we love and serve God with all our heart, we will never know an end to our happiness.

(A more complete list of such life-lessons appears in my book, *Upbringing: A Discussion Handbook for Parents*, also published by Scepter.)

There are no set formulas, no typical situations, for teaching these and other truths to your children. The key thing is that you understand and believe them yourself, that they form the base for your judgment and ethics. When this happens, the lessons surface spontaneously in your conversation, especially when you lead your children to understand people and values, and most especially when you help them learn from mistakes.

Values

You can teach your children values by teaching them priorities in life, for this is what "values" means: what comes first, second, third and so on, in our will and affections—what lies closest to our heart.

Help your children to understand people, something they must do to make their ways in life. They should grasp what motivates people, and how differences in motives make for strong or weak character, honorable or dishonorable behavior. So much of life is really a question of heart.

They should understand what a hero is: a person who, even with personal flaws and shortcomings, embodies the virtues—one who accomplishes great things through the fulfillment of responsibility.

All the saints of the past are heroes to us, as are the saints of the present.

You can use characters of literature, movies, history, and biography to teach about people's values. You can do the same with living figures from the present, but always, of course, with charity. If we find something regrettable in people's lives, it is the *fault* we deplore, not the *person*. A Christian bears no personal ill will toward anyone, no matter what the provocation. If Christ could love and forgive his executioners, we can love and forgive anyone.

So, on those occasions when you can speak with your children about values, the priorities in life, you can use this framework. Looking at a character in literature or history or the movies, reflect on what seems to be this person's order of wants and ambitions. From the following list of loves and desires, which mean the most to the person, and in which order?

- God
- family and friends
- country
- money
- fame/glory
- satisfying work
- job advancement
- comfort and convenience
- pleasure and amusement
- power over others
- safety and security
- conformity: acceptance by others
- vengeance

The saints put God first, and the martyrs put him ahead of life itself—like St. Thomas More, who gave up office, family, friends, and all the comforts of life rather than offend God. The missionaries put God ahead of family, country, money, and comfort; to them nothing was more important than winning souls for God.

Other heroes put love for family, friends, and country ahead of wealth, power, and security. Some men today put God and family before money and job advancement, declining a promotion that would mean moving to another city and thus disrupting their children's education; in a quiet way, they are heroic. Every day, dedicated wives and mothers put God and family ahead of comfort, convenience, amusement, and conformity; they too are heroes. So also are those parents who give their children brothers and sisters rather than toys and gadgets, money and comfort; courageously, they love God and family first.

Sad to say, other people put power ahead of everything, and they are often elected to public office. Others value pleasure and comfort before God and family; they hold no religious faith, and their marriages are a wreck. Still others abandon their parents' faith rather than appear "different"; they put conformity and security before God and family.

The list of lives with misplaced values could go on and on, not just from literature and television but from the folks in our neighborhood or workplace.

Evaluating people like this will help your children understand the meaning of *principles*—the absolutely first place that we give to God and his moral law, and consequently the iron determination we hold to put family, friends, truth, and justice ahead of everything else whatsoever.

This habitual way of assessing people's motives, their principles or lack thereof, is necessary for your children's shrewdness later in life. It helps them understand, for instance, why you may disapprove of certain companions of theirs and insist on their breaking off relations: "We have nothing personal against Johnny. . . . It's just that, unfortunately, he and his family do not share our principles; and good friends should share principles."

It will lead them to make wise choices about the people they associate with later—friends, bosses and co-workers, teachers and coaches, university professors—and that most important choice of all, one's spouse.

Young people on the verge of marriage should look closely at many traits in a prospective spouse, but the most important is whether he or she shares one's principles. Husband and wife may differ in a number of areas, but they must have the same principled values. Your children will be able to evaluate a prospective spouse's principles only if they clearly know their own. In a real sense, this is one of the surest ways to prepare them for a permanent, stable, and happy marriage.

Learning from mistakes

It should be clear that your job as a parent is to raise your children to become men and women of purposeful action. They should grow to be confident people, as energetic as their temperament allows. They should habitually set and strive for goals. (People cannot really strive for ideals in life unless they also strive for goals, small and large, near and distant.)

They should have an enterprising spirit, willing and able to take calculated risks and then live with the consequences. In short, they should someday become leaders, both in the workplace and in their own families.

Bear in mind that your highly energetic two-year-old son, relentlessly exploring everywhere in your house and driving you crazy, can grow to be a vigorous, clear-sighted professional man and father who inspires confidence among clients, colleagues, and his children. That headstrong little daughter of yours, cagey and charmingly assertive, can someday be a great wife and mother, a respected professional, and a charismatic leader in her community. Your job is to direct your children's energies and strengthen their judgment, so they will someday give glory to God. They will be producers, not "consumers."

If you raise your children to live this way, as confident risk-takers, then you can expect them to make mistakes along the way, a good many mistakes. This is normal, natural, even healthy.

After all, you do not want your children to be fearful and inert. Lazy, timid conformists seldom make active mistakes; their great errors are those of negligence, which are usually the worst of all—especially in raising children and fulfilling other important duties. This way of life is not for your sons and daughters.

In other words, there is nothing wrong with your children's making mistakes as they grow up if two things hold true. First, that they *try* to do the right thing, for you expect an earnest "best effort" from them, not perfection or results. Secondly, that they learn from their mistakes, reflect on what went wrong and why so as to avoid another fall.

People who learn from their mistakes grow steadily and rapidly in sound judgment. Experience leads to confident competence. It also leads to respect for other people's experience, which is one of the hallmarks of professionalism.

So you, as a parent, will see your children make misjudgments in family life, in school, and in their athletics. They may botch up doing a chore. They may copy down a homework assignment incorrectly and thus do the wrong lesson. They may miss a ball passed to them in a soccer game because they were distracted. They may blurt out a remark to a friend and thus cause offense. They may lose track of time when visiting a friend and then arrive home late. They may borrow something from a sibling without permission and then accidentally break it. They may ignore parents' advice about something and then get into trouble. The list goes on and on. . . .

Even though your family life is busy, though you have a hundred things to do a day, it is worth your effort to talk with your children and help them learn from these errors. This is one of the best investments of time you can make. There are no formulas for this sort of discussion, of course, but certain approaches seem to work effectively.

First, though you can point out the mistake on the spot, call your child's serious attention to it, you should strive to make the corrective discussion privately and personally, even if this means waiting a few minutes or (with older children) a couple of hours. Private discussion sinks in more deeply; your child is not distracted and resentful, and embarrassed by others listening in. This is especially important if you are upset by the mistake. Put off the discussion, if possible, until you have cooled down and can think more calmly.

Secondly, do your best to determine whether your child was really trying to do the right thing. A so-called "honest mistake"—an error committed while attempting to act rightly—is far less serious than careless negligence or mean-spirited impulse. Ask about it: "Did you *try* to do this right?" Let your children see how highly you always value their good intention (which makes up, in part, their integrity).

Finally, if you can, lead them in retrospect through what they did, helping them to see where they went wrong. Ask them:

- What were you thinking when you did this? What did you expect to happen?
- What exactly went wrong?
- What was your reaction? What did you think and feel?
- What did people around you say and do? How did your mistake affect them?
- If your mistake caused a problem or offense to someone else, how do you think they feel right now?
- What can you do now to repair this mistake? If you offended someone, even without meaning to, don't you think you should say you're sorry?
- If you're ever in this situation again, what will you do differently? What have you learned?

If you lead your children often enough through this sort of reflection, they will form a habit of thinking this way. Some good will come from their mistakes, for their judgment and self-honesty will be stronger. Perhaps most importantly, they will be less inclined to blame others for their falls and, when offended themselves, will be more ready to extend understanding and forgiveness.

Reflect on this: How many marriages would be strengthened, even saved, by each spouse's honesty in admitting mistakes and asking forgiveness from the other? And, of course, with its corollary—patience with the other spouse's mistakes and quickness to forgive, forget, and move on? When you struggle to *change yourself first*, not the other,

you become a better spouse and parent. Truth leads to justice, and justice strengthens love. One of the most beautiful
phrases in family life is "I'm sorry. . . . please forgive me."

Christianity vs. materialism

Broadly speaking, what you are really teaching is the difference between Christian truth, a Christ-centered vision of
life, and the life-outlook of materialism.

Materialism is not merely the pursuit of things. It is,
rather, *to see man as a thing*—an intelligent primate, a beast—
and *to treat other people as mere objects*, valued only in terms of
our power and pleasure. Materialism denotes several beliefs:
there is no God; life ends with death; we answer to no one
but the law for the way we live; "truth" is relative; "conscience" is shapeless sentimentality; morality is only social
convention; the only real evil is physical pain and discomfort;
life's purpose is the maximum pursuit of pleasure and power.

This life-outlook permeates our society, and indeed
dominated societies of the pre-Christian era. It is the Great
Lie of our time. It is the latest form of the original temptation in Genesis (3: 5): "You shall be like gods. . . ." History
shows that those who seek to live like gods, without limits or
answerability, wind up living like beasts. The Great Lie, sown
by the Evil One, shows itself at work all around us. In the
United States each year, more than a million women pay
someone to kill their unborn children. Abortion mills are
listed in the Yellow Pages. Legal, socially accepted pornography treats men and women like swine. Families rip apart
through selfish conflict, and children's hearts are broken.

Breadwinners are unjustly fired, their livelihoods needlessly sacrificed for higher profits. Talk shows blabber shamelessly about the belly and groin, and celebrities discuss everything except those questions at the center of life—What happens after we die? What is the meaning of suffering? To whom do we answer for the way we live?

In the midst of this reckless bestiality, your mission is to teach your children the truth, the Christian faith at the center of our hearts: We are beloved children of God. We were enslaved by sin, but he redeemed us through his Son. We answer to him for the way we live. We offend him and damage our souls by choosing something contrary to his will. He left himself in his Church to missionize and save us through the generations of history. We are responsible for the souls around us. This life is a transitory phase, and each of us shall either live forever in heaven or suffer the "second death" for eternity. We shall never be really happy unless we strive to serve God with all our heart, soul, mind, and strength.

If this Christian faith underlies your lessons of right and wrong, your children will adopt it and live by it all their lives. Your voice will be their conscience. They will know materialism when they see it around them. They will shun it and deflect it from their own families. They, like you, will die to themselves—will endure any sacrifice—before permitting it to corrupt their children.

May you someday know the deep happiness St. John described in his third epistle (verse 4): "I have no greater joy than to hear that my children are walking in the truth."

6

Responsibility, Courage, Self-Mastery

IN THE LAST CHAPTER, we saw how children's minds are formed to know right from wrong, to recognize the great truths in life as the light for their future lives. In this chapter, we focus more on the will and heart—the desire to do the right thing (once we judge what it is) and the strength to carry it out, to put it into action. Thus we discuss the virtues of responsibility, courageous perseverance, and self-mastery.

The religious upbringing of your children depends on all these strengths. As we said before, good intentions are not enough. Grace builds on nature, and God will depend on your children's strong character to carry out his will effectively all their lives and lead others to do the same— starting with their families and radiating out to the rest of society.

You may instruct your children in the catechism; but if they grow up weak, irresolute, and habitually self-indulgent, they will never amount to anything. They may know what is right but lack the courage to live rightly. They may know what is wrong but collapse in the face of temptation. Superficial pious practices are no substitute for strength of character. God and his Church need valiant men and women, and it is your sacred mission to produce them.

Responsibility

The word "responsibility" is related to "respond," and it implies the existence of another, someone to whom we answer. We answer to another in authority (God, parents, teachers, employers, the law) for the way we conduct our lives, for the way we treat others.

The whole of children's moral development comes down to this: moving from self to others. Small children are self-centered; responsible adults are other-centered. Children are led out of preoccupation with self to respect for, and service of, the rights and needs of others.

The existence of other people's rights (something children must learn) leads to our obligations. God has a right to be obeyed and worshiped, so we have the duty to do this. People on the highway have a right to physical safety, so we are obligated to drive carefully. Parents have given us life in all the rich meanings of the word, and so we are bound to honor them forever.

This virtue, like that of sound judgment, is rich and all-encompassing. Its meaning embraces so much of life that perhaps we can describe it more easily than define it. We know responsible people when we meet them in life. Who are they?

Responsible people center their lives on service to others, not preoccupation with their own power. Their eyes are on the needs of others, not themselves. A responsible public official considers the welfare of his country. A responsible professional thinks of clients and customers. A responsible husband dedicates himself to his wife. A responsible wife devotes herself to her husband. They both sacrifice themselves for their children.

Responsible people carry out their duties thoroughly whether they feel like it or not. Professionalism, so they say, is the ability to do our best work no matter how we feel. Responsible parents carry out their family obligations even when they are tired and tempted to slacken; they never let up, and they never give up.

Responsible people live with the consequences of their free decisions and mistakes. They answer for what they do. They do not lie to themselves and shift blame to others; they do not view themselves as victims.

Responsible people honor their promises and commitments, no matter what sacrifice this involves.

Responsible people mind their own business; they do not meddle in matters that do not concern them. They refrain from gossip, detraction, and rash judgment. They give other people the benefit of doubt and respect people's right to presumption of innocence.

Responsible people grasp the relationship between negligence and harm, and this moves them to act rightly. To neglect one's duty, whatever it may be, causes damage or offense to others. A slipshod surgeon can cripple his patient. A reckless driver can kill his passengers. A negligent parent can destroy his or her children.

Responsible people acknowledge and respect the rightful authority of others. They respect God's law and the civil law, as well as the rights of teachers and bosses. By learning how to obey, they learn how to command. Though they do not dwell overmuch on their rights, they know what these are, and they are prepared to defend them against injustice.

Responsible people are excellent citizens, workers, and parents. They are the building blocks of healthy families and society.

Responsibility is, in other words, another term for *love*. Real love is not just sweet sentiments. It is the conscientious drive to carry out our duties—to God, family, neighbors, country—to the point of sacrifice.

This kind of love is found in every great family.

Teaching responsibility

How can you, as a parent, teach this life-outlook to your children? Many of the ways have already been suggested. Let us look at them again and consider still other approaches.

The theme of personal responsibility runs all through the rules for the home outlined in Chapter 4. Each rule, if carried out consistently and repeatedly, draws children out of their selfish concerns and leads them to serve God and the rest of the family. Since the rules start with "we"—that is, since they bind parents as well as children—the parents give ongoing personal example of responsibility.

This purposeful example-giving is important, especially these days. Bear in mind that children today seldom see their parents, especially their father, live on-the-job responsibility. Home life today is heavily, almost exclusively, devoted to leisure pursuits, amusement, and entertainment. In the children's experience, therefore, life is mostly play. The world of serious work, where nearly all adults exercise their powers most fully and responsibly, lies entirely outside children's vision and therefore their lesson-learning experience. So, if parents do not purposely show responsible behavior at home, and insist that their children follow suit, then the children fail to understand the concept. They never see it in action.

Responsible parents frequently draw their children's attention to the greatness of the other spouse. Children need to be reminded: Mom and Dad honor each other. Mom says, for instance, "See how patient and dedicated your father is, how much he loves us; see how he goes off to work even when he is tired or has a headache." Dad, in turn, says, "Your mother is a great woman. See how she never stops serving us, doing countless things for our happiness, no matter how tired she is. She deserves the best that we can give her."

If children respect their parents, they will unconsciously imitate them. A huge part of that respect (as with any respect given another) derives from one's "reputation." So each parent works, on purpose, to reinforce the other's "reputation"—the high esteem earned by personal excellence.

In a healthy family, moreover, the children feel needed. Each of them has household chores to do, large or small, by which they serve the whole family. Even when the jobs involve their personal affairs (cleaning their rooms, putting away toys, making their beds in the morning), they are contributing to the appearance and order of the home, something the parents value highly and therefore insist upon. Later in life, children cannot take care of others (the mark of real maturity) without prior years of practice in managing their own affairs.

This includes the children's home assignments for school. Parents make clear they expect personal best effort, not just top grades. If the children are evidently doing their best, that is enough for Mom and Dad. But here, as in other areas of family life, the children must try and they must expend serious effort.

The children naturally need standards made clear to them. One way parents do this is to check over the children's written homework. Does it look hastily done? Are there careless spelling mistakes? If we read the work aloud (an excellent practice in family life), can we spot grammatical glitches and faulty logic? Since schoolwork is really a long-term preparation for professional work, the children need to learn habitual standards of neatness and clear expression. Therefore, if the schoolwork is substandard, then parents make the children redo it—which is standard practice in any quality workplace.

Effective parents know the importance of encouragement and sincere praise in family life. In one form or other, they press their children to outdo themselves, to focus their strengths on a task at hand. (All responsibility is, after all, a call for us to outdo ourselves.) They let the children try tasks by themselves. That is, they *direct* the children, giving advice and suggestions until the children have clearly done their best. Only then do they step in and help to finish the task if necessary. Parents use phrases such as. . . .

- You're not a baby anymore. . . . You can do it your-
  self. . . .
- I know you can do it if you try. . . .
- You're stronger than you think. . . .
- Don't give up yet. . . . Try it again. . . .
- You're almost there; try it one more time. . . .
- Don't be a quitter. . . .
- You did your best, and I'm proud of you.

"I'm proud of you"—How much this phrase means to children! Children need encouraging praise as much as correction, and praise should be as specific as blame. The praise should be focused on their earnest attempts to do a job right, regardless of outcome; you are pleased that they try their best. And certainly, when the job is well done, you give them the honest praise they have earned.

Praise must be sincere, of course, for children are acutely sensitive to phoniness; they see right through it. In some ways, insincere and undeserved praise is worse than none at all. Children, like all the rest of us, discount a judgment that is clearly exaggerated. Here, as in so many other aspects of family life, love for the truth is paramount.

Courageous perseverance

The discussion above about responsibility leads naturally into, and indeed overlaps, our considering the virtue of fortitude. It takes great strength of will and heart to carry out responsibilities, and this strength is vital for children's growth in character.

How can we understand fortitude? What characterizes people with this virtue?

Courageous people have an acquired ability to *overcome* or *endure* difficulties. They can withstand inconvenience and even physical pain. They recover quickly from setbacks and disappointments.

Courageous people can endure the tedium that much of life necessarily entails. When motivated by love or some high ideal, they can stick with some routine task as long as necessary: changing diapers, washing laundry, preparing meals, commuting back and forth to school or workplace, processing repeated tasks at the office—the repeated cycles of duty in normal daily life. To submit oneself to routine this way, out of love, takes courage. (How many marriages break apart because one or both spouses, raised to see life as a succession of amusements, cannot bear normal routine in life?)

Courageous people live by a simple principle: If we do not work to control events, then they control us.

Courageous people are realistically confident of their problem-solving abilities. In their upbringing, they had plenty of practice in solving problems. Consequently they habitually turn anxiety into purposeful, honorable action. They are neither worrywarts nor whiners, but rather people who get things done.

Courageous people see *escape* as something unworthy of them, even dishonorable. They are undeterred by fear. Though they may be afraid in a tough situation, they do not let fear paralyze them. Courage is the power to act even when we are afraid.

Courageous people are not quitters. They keep trying long after others would give up. They do not apply one or two tries to a challenge, but rather five, ten, or twenty tries, or more. In this sense, courageous people sometimes appear "unreasonable." As someone once said, mankind's greatest achievements have been accomplished by "unreasonable" people.

Teaching fortitude

The previous section about teaching responsibility shows how parents encourage children in their duties. Honest praise does wonders to build children's confident perseverance. In a real sense, *children build self-confidence upon their parents' confidence in them.* Children sense that their parents have high expectations for their performance, high hopes in their growing powers, and they gradually grow up to these standards.

Remember: Children either grow *up* to our expectations, or *down* to them. So, your children need to hear from you, over and again: "You're stronger than you think. . . . I know you're not a quitter. . . . I have confidence in you. . . . I'm proud of you." This applies to all the challenges your youngsters face at home, in school, and in sports.

Athletics are enormously helpful for teaching your children strength of will, personal courage. Through persistent encouragement, parents and coaches teach children how to handle physical pain and discomfort, setbacks and disappointment, temptations to give up. The whole dynamic of team sports teaches youngsters to collaborate with others, to assess their own strengths and limitations realistically, and to appreciate other people's best efforts.

All of these benefits depend on proper coaching, of course. Coaches with a "win at all costs" mentality should be avoided. Winning is *not* everything. If it were, George Washington would have been fired during the American Revolution, and St. Paul would have quit after his missionary failure in Athens.

To strive honorably to win, to put forth our best efforts in service to our team, to give our heart to our team even when we sit out games on the sidelines, to learn from mistakes and bounce back from losses—this is everything. The best coaches think and act this way. Indeed the very best coaches are passionately dedicated to their players' growth in character.

If you find a coach like this, you should treasure him or her as a great family friend, a solid support to your formative efforts at home. If you cannot find such a coach, maybe you can become one yourself. The time and energy this requires is, to be sure, a sacrifice. But your children are youngsters only once. All the rest of their lives, they would remember how much you taught them about life through your patient coaching. It is worth a try.

Another area for growth in courage is resistance to peer pressures, a healthy indifference to being "different." Your children must learn one important lesson about life when they are young: "Everybody else is doing it" is a lame reason for doing anything.

Though some social conformity is necessary and normal, conformity itself is no substitute for conscience. In the area of moral living, doing good and shunning evil, public opinion has no value whatever. Pilate clearly knew Jesus was innocent, but he caved in before raucous public opinion and a threat to his job. Peter denied he knew Jesus rather than look bad before a small crowd huddled by a fire; he spent the rest of his life repenting this cowardice.

A conscientious Christian has always been, and will always be, at least slightly "different" from others in a materialistic society. This takes courage.

When your children are in their teens, they will be enticed to try drugs. This is a certainty; it will happen. When it happens, your children will need the courage to resist. They will need such a strong conscience—the voice of God speaking through their memory of your lessons—that they will endure anything rather than offend their Savior and betray your trust in them.

When they are away at college, they may be the only students in their dorm living a chaste life. And for this they may be ridiculed. They can withstand this if they have a lifelong habit of right living, a healthy indifference to wrongful conformity. A Christian needs a clean heart and a thick skin.

Therefore, a maxim for children when they are young: "Sticks and stones may break my bones, but names will never hurt me."

So, when your children ask for some fad (some fashionable clothes or toy or gadget) because "everyone else has one," tell them this is not a good enough reason. Think about, and lead them to see, the relative merits of the thing desired. Do they *need* this? What for? What will happen if they do not have one—and is this judgment a guess or a fact?

Is it really worth the price? (Most fad items are, of course, overpriced.) What will happen if we wait a few weeks before buying?

Certainly, no hard and fast rule applies here. Buying some "in" clothes and gadgets (if you can afford this) is harmless in itself. What counts here is the children's *reason*. We may buy fashionable things for any number of reasons—because of need, quality, and price, for instance—but not quickly and not because we blindly follow the crowd.

All other things being equal, it is healthy to make your children *wait* for things, and if possible to *earn* them. Children learn the real value of things by waiting and earning. A healthy family thus avoids impulse purchases. You can and should occasionally splurge on treats to eat, a good movie, a night out for dinner, and the like. But this is to please the family or its guests. For other purchases, make the children wait. (Who knows? Since most fads today have the life span of a fruit fly, you may wait until the fad has faded into history. That, too, would be a lesson for your children.)

Self-mastery

Unfortunately, the word "temperance" has come on hard times in our era. It has had a so-called "bad press." People generally associate the word with prudish, self-righteous campaigns against alcohol. Too bad, because this is not what the virtue of temperance means at all. This strength is, in fact, among the qualities we admire most in people. It characterizes great leaders and esteemed friends.

Temperance means self-mastery, a steady control over our lower appetites and passions, including our tendencies to laziness, complacency, and reluctance to carry out responsibility. As such it is intimately bound up with the virtue of fortitude.

In a broad sense, youngsters are "tempered" the way steel is tempered, and for the same reasons. Raw iron is subjected to pressure and friction, purposeful adversity, to shape it into a strong and supple instrument capable of competent service.

Related to this—and most happily—temperance also means enjoying the good things of life in moderation, never to excess. It means being on top of life, living life as richly and beautifully as God intended when he made us.

We know temperate, self-controlled people when we meet them, for they make wonderful friends. They are a delight to be with and to live with.

Temperate people enjoy all the good gifts of life in balanced moderation. They like food, drink, entertainment, recreation, work itself. They are confident people, so they do not overindulge in these things. (Insecure people are the ones who overeat, addict themselves to pleasure, and work to excess from unreasonable fear of failure.)

Temperate people know how to say "no" to themselves, or at least "later." They are patient with themselves and others. They can delay gratification at will; they can casually take or leave enjoyable goods. At a party, they can nurse one drink all night. At dinner, they give the best to guests. At the office, they can work hard all day without letup, then quit and go home at a reasonable hour. They can set aside the newspaper to help children with homework. They wait for rewards and know they must earn them.

Temperate people know how to concentrate on a task. They have the practiced power to work quickly without hurrying, and carefully without dawdling. They can set and meet their own deadlines. They see time as a resource, not a passive environment.

Temperate people make good bosses and get promoted. They are assertive but not obnoxiously aggressive. They give people direction, not just orders. They take responsibilities seriously, but they are good humored as well and enjoy a good laugh. Being confident leaders, they have devoted followers. People enjoy working with them.

Temperate people put people ahead of things. (Insecure people do the opposite.) When enjoying themselves—with meals, drink, sports, games—their enjoyment derives from their company, the people with them, not the activities themselves. They delight in delighting their friends.

Temperate people are not coarse in speech, for such talk is a kind of impulsive self-indulgence and shows disrespect for one's company.

Temperate people habitually are courteous to everyone, even in the face of provocation. *Please* and *thank you* and *excuse me* punctuate their speech. They are not interrupters. They are slow to anger, quick to forgive and forget. They never indulge in nursing grudges.

In a word, temperate people have "class." Their dealings with others are marked by etiquette, healthy self-respect, active concern for the dignity and needs of others, an active spirit of service. For all these traits, they earn the esteem of friends and even the grudging respect of adversaries. People trust them and their judgment. Consequently they get promoted and elected to positions of responsibility. They are leaders.

May God grant you the reward of seeing your children grow up this way.

Teaching self-control: some principles

Several practical principles hold true here, and you should always bear them in mind—especially when you think you are going to lose your mind.

- Your strategy is not to *control* the children; it is to form in them the *lifelong habit of controlling themselves.*

- This vitally important task takes years to accomplish, but not so long as you may think. The toughest time, by far, is when they are two to five years old, the wildest time of life. If you can instill good habits and attitudes in them by age six, you are more than half-way to victory.

- In any house with small children, there is a power struggle going on: Who is the boss around here? The child aggressively seeks to dominate, and the conscientious parent is determined this will not happen. The parents are in control of the home, period. If you win in this struggle, if your children emerge at age six with this clear understanding and submission, they will have confidence in you and peace of mind. You can then direct them effectively for the rest of their years under your roof, even in adolescence.

- The key lessons to teach small children are these:

(a) respect for you and your rightful authority, (b) respect for the rights of others, (c) habits of personal piety, gratitude to God. These are vital for your children's learning everything else you must teach them, now and later.

- Other lessons need to be taught as well: personal order and cleanliness, good manners, eating habits, and the like. You can begin to teach these under age six, but this will enjoy only moderate success at best—fits and starts, progress and reverses, endless repetition, sometimes no signs of progress at all. Be patient and persevering. As long as the children are learning the key lessons about authority and rights and piety, all the other lessons are just crude basics, a foundation for later development. After age six, the children will make much more rapid progress in all areas—just as a skyscraper builds up quickly once its solid foundation is laid.

- You can always count on God's help, for you are doing what he put you on earth to do—to fashion each of your children into the masterpiece he had in mind when he entrusted them to your care. You have the right to ask him for an occasional miracle. But remember, his miracles often required some prior sacrifice and unpleasantries—spittle in the ear, mud smeared on eyes, a storm at sea, a fruitless search for fish, the tearful pleas of parents. He asks you what he asked these people: Where is your faith?

- Have faith in God and in your ultimate victory. If you keep at the struggle and never give up, no matter what, your ongoing mistakes and reverses will not matter. At some point, sooner perhaps than you think, your children will show signs of really growing up: they will bring you honor with their conscience, conduct, and character.

The body

Before discussing how successful parents teach temperance at home, we must consider an important matter: the influence of body chemistry on children's emotions.

Children, like adults, are not disembodied spirits. They have a physical body that is powerfully influenced by biochemistry. Mood swings and crankiness, irrational fears and aggressiveness, sluggishness and baseless melancholy—all these emotional states can derive in huge measure from the complex interactions of one's brain and glands.

Specialists say that the age from two to five, a period of rapid bodily growth and development, is characterized by intense biochemical activity. The same reagents that cause bodily changes also affect a child's emotions, often in dramatic and unpleasant ways. This dynamic, essentially out of anyone's control, accounts in large part for small children's occasional displays of near-lunatic behavior. (By the way, the same phenomenon reappears in early adolescence, where once again the body undergoes rapid development.)

Parents who are aware of this situation concentrate on their small children's bodily health. The children need nutritious diets, not gobs of junk food. They need plenty of healthy exercise, not trance-like lassitude in front of a television set. They need plenty of sleep, for most bodily development apparently takes place during sleep, and a lack of sufficient sleep makes children irritable. (Adults, too. A great many frictions in modern family life can be traced to insufficient exercise and sleep.)

Moreover, since we inherit our bodies from forebears, some children apparently inherit genetic problems with their biochemistry. They may be highly sensitive to sugar, for instance. Pastries, soft drinks, and other sweets may act as psychoactive drugs on them, leading to swings between aggressive elation and sad irritability as well as difficulties in concentration. This genetic sensitivity (to sugar or other foodstuffs) may affect only one child in a family, much as one redhead may appear among dark-haired siblings.

Parents who face such a situation should consult medical specialists for direction. This is especially important if either parent has a family history of addictive behavior: alcoholism, substance abuse, heavy smoking, excessive and compulsive caffeine consumption. Medical science is now fairly certain that addictive behavior has some sort of genetic basis. Many "problem children" may be suffering from undetected and undiagnosed medical dysfunctions. Their genetically based problems are made drastically worse by a loose, unstructured family life, one given over to self-indulgence and TV-induced sensory stimulation.

In any event, all children benefit from healthy habits of bodily self-control. Keeping the TV under control leads to healthy exercise and more time for restful sleep. Saying "no" to between-meal snacks leads to better appetite and more nourishing food intake. A balance of work, play, and sleep leads to more equanimity and peace of mind. In large measure, temperance means control of one's body, and this begins when the children are small.

A parenthesis here, related to the above: If you are frazzled and exhausted by mid-morning or at any other time of the day, and maybe notice yourself irritably overreacting to your children's antics, take a look at your caffeine intake. Two or three cups of coffee for breakfast or lunch could account for some of your angry confrontations. It takes two to have an argument, and maybe you are partly at fault. Cut back on your caffeine or cut it out for a few weeks and see what happens. Many parents have tried this and found significant improvement. Temperance, like charity, begins at home.

Leadership in temperance

All this being said, let us look at how effective parents teach their children the character strength of temperance. Some of these have already appeared in our discussion of the other virtues.

"Time management" is another term for self-control. So, a temperate home is a structured one. Parents establish set routines for rising, meals, sports and recreation, homework, and going to bed. At any given time, children should know what they ought to be doing. Your ongoing control of the family schedule and rules leads to the children's sense of security and, consequently, their confidence in you as a competent leader.

To be sure, they will occasionally resist your direction. They will push to take control—to watch TV instead of doing chores and homework, to stay up past bedtime, to leave toys scattered about, to lie in bed late or watch mindless cartoons on Saturday morning. You do not let them take control. *You do not accept their "no," but they must accept yours.* Effective parenting is largely the power to resist children's resistance and to keep at this until, eventually, they submit to your loving leadership.

Leading the children to live by the house's rules naturally leads to practice of self-control. Allowing no quarrels at dinner teaches self-restraint. The same holds true for limits on phone-time. Some families also have a custom of the "job jar." This is a jar or box with slips of paper describing jobs and repairs needed around the house. Any child who complains of being bored is directed to the job jar: pick out three tasks and choose one—then go do it. Families with this custom almost never hear children's complaints about boredom, having "nothing to do."

Here is another way to look at it: Boredom nearly always derives from stagnancy. That is, some power of mind or body is going unchallenged and unexercised. Physically active adults grow bored with a sedentary job. Imaginative, artistic people are slowly tortured by dull routine. Socially active people languish when alone. To be agonized by boredom is to hear the voice of some powers within us pleading, "Put us to work, will you?"

The last thing children need in family life is pointless idleness, which is often disguised as protracted amusement. Children need occasional healthy recreation, as everyone does, for recreation has a purpose: it "re-creates" our energies, restores us to the health we need to get on with life.

Idleness and extended amusements do not fulfill this function. They are flights from boredom, not rest from work, and lead children to see time as an enemy instead of a resource. Children raised with this attitude live too much in the ever-present "now." They want and expect pleasant sensations right now.

Children need to manage time, to get control of their own affairs. Therefore, as your children approach adolescence, ages eleven to thirteen, they should learn to use a personal calendar. They should keep a notebook for homework assignments, appointments, and other time-marked duties. You should oversee how effectively they do this. The ability to plan ahead and pace oneself toward a deadline is one mark of maturity. To control oneself means, among other things, the power to control one's time.

It also means to control one's finances. One of the main causes for lives of excess among older children and teens is that they have too much money. You can help your children live temperately by constraining them to live within reasonable means. That is, give them enough pocket money to cover their weekly needs—bus fare, school expenses, soft drink with friends after sports—plus a little extra, say 15 percent. If they need cash for a larger purchase, they come and ask for it; this is the occasion for discussing how wise the expense really is.

Should you give them a regular allowance? There's no pat answer for this. Some parents prefer to give a fixed amount per week and then let the children budget expenses. Others prefer that children come for cash when they need it. Either method seems to work, depending on the parents' temperament and time constraints. Whichever approach parents are comfortable with, and therefore confident about, seems to work fine.

The key idea is to hold disposable income to a minimum. This keeps kids from turning wants and whimsical fads into needs. Our society has too many immature adults stuck in a permanent adolescence, treating all their income as "spending money." Your children should not grow up this way.

Another area is your relentless teaching about manners. You and your spouse use *please, thank you,* and *excuse me* in family life, and you insist that your children do the same. With small children, this requires seemingly endless repetition. Be assured, it is not endless. At some point, the children form the habit; they will use the terms naturally, most of the time, in their speech. From that point on, your corrections will be merely reminders. (We all need occasional reminding, even in adulthood, of what we know to be true.) These terms of politeness are a ramp up to the children's grasp of moral truth: that other people have dignity and rights.

Bear in mind also that these terms are a basis for our dealings with God. All our loving prayers to God come down, one way or another, to *please, thank you, I'm sorry,* and *I give my word*—petition, thanksgiving, repentance, and resolution. Courtesy in the family leads to courtesy with our heavenly Father. As St. John put it (I John 4: 20), "For how can he who does not love his brother, whom he sees, love God, whom he does not see?"

Related to this is the family custom of shunning gossip and personal negative criticism. We do not speak ill of people behind their backs, for this is unjust and uncharitable. When we speak of public officials, we may deplore their policies and act to remove them from office, but we bear them no personal animosity. We pray for the President, for he too has a soul, and his rightful authority comes from God. This is what we have been taught by Christ and Sts. Peter and Paul.

A temperate Christian parent also oversees what comes into the home and uses this to teach lessons of moral discernment. If a TV program shows something lewd or gratuitously violent, you walk to the set and turn it off. If a magazine displays some soft-porn pictures, you rip them out and even cancel the subscription. If a music tape contains suggestive lyrics, you discard it.

Is this censorship? Sure it is, and there is nothing wrong with it. If publishers and producers can choose what to present, you certainly can choose what to accept. The customer is always right. It is your home, no one else's, and therefore you have a right to the last word on the matter.

Some canny parents also use what may be called "directed overhearing." That is, they purposely discuss some subject with each other that they want the children, especially older ones, to overhear. This is done in those circumstances where everyone is together: at meals, driving in a car, sitting around the living room. For instance, the news that day describes a fatal car crash involving teenagers. The parents comment on it: "What a tragedy. . . . We should pray for them and their poor families. . . . I wonder if the cause was alcohol or (more likely) just impulsive showing off. . . . If the driver survived, imagine how he'll feel for the rest of his life, knowing he caused someone's death. . . . What a difference one bad judgment, a single minute of reckless-ness, can make in a person's life. . . ." This is not a bogus discussion, of course; it is real and sincere. But it conveys a lesson sideways, as it were, to the children who overhear. Though they do not get a lecture, they get the point.

Fun and friendship

Much of our discussion on temperance up to now has centered on negative matters, setting limits on children's ten-dencies to excess. This is necessary. But of course, temper-ance also means enjoyment. It means healthy fun.

Don Giovanni Bosco, the patron saint of youth, used to give some excellent advice to the young people in his care: "Always remain in the state of grace . . . and enjoy life as much as you can!"

Temperate men and women are serious of purpose but light in touch. They take their responsibilities seriously, but not themselves. No one enjoys life more than a saint. And no one makes a better friend.

Teach your children to enjoy life, but never past the point of offending God and others. Lead them to see that the good things in life—delicious food and drink, quality films and programs, sports and recreation, challenging work, even a good night's sleep—are all gifts from God. He enjoys seeing his children happy, as all good parents do.

God has arranged human nature such that the greatest happiness comes with moderation, that midpoint between two extremes. Not enough food makes us hungry and irritable; too much makes us bloated and chubby. Not enough work makes us bored; too much exhausts us. Not enough reading and viewing makes us dull; too much leads us to neglect our exercise. Not enough sports exercise makes us flabby and sluggish; too much leads us to neglect our mind and duties. We are happiest when we enjoy these goods as God intended, right in the middle.

Your children need to see you living by this standard. Good food and drink, sports and games, movies and shows, cookouts and parties—all should be part of family life, in balance with the family's responsibilities.

Recreation should serve to "re-create" our powers, not exhaust them; we re-energize ourselves so as to better tackle our duties. Leisure is a spice of life, not its main course.

You have to decide with your spouse how much is enough, for there are no hard and fast standards. There are some clues, though, that things are going too far and need to be scaled back or drastically overhauled—

- Children are growing soft and slightly overweight from snacks and sedentary inertia.
- Homework and chores are neglected for lack of time or energy.
- Mom is frazzled from chauffeuring kids back and forth to activities.
- Children's conversation centers on shows and entertainers, fashions and gadgets; the children talk like apprentice consumers.
- Children are tired out from sports rather than calmly energized.

- Music drowns out or substitutes for family conversation.
- Background noise from video games or music becomes an annoying distraction.
- Older children seldom plan more than a couple of days ahead.

One parental rule of thumb: If you intuitively sense that some activity is overdone, it probably is. If it begins to bother you, even vaguely, it has probably gone too far already. Time for action. Scale it back or shut it down.

When a family's leisure activities are enjoyed in moderation, they become all the more valued. Relative rarity makes anything more valuable, whether gold or stamps or coins— or TV shows, ball games, snacks, or spending money.

Every family needs occasional recreation. This is true of any group engaged in a serious enterprise. Our Lord himself lived this way. In one Gospel scene, we recall, his disciples were so busy coming and going that they hardly had time to eat. Our Savior said, "Let us come apart and rest a while." In effect: Let's drop everything. . . . We need a break.

In other words, there is such a thing as legitimate splurging. Part of being a good leader, including a good parent, is to know when and how to make sensible exceptions. An occasional spontaneous treat in family life is necessary, and it binds everyone closer together.

This leads us to one of the most crucial lesson to teach your children: the importance of friends.

Temperance centers essentially on the welfare of others, not ourselves. Self-controlled people are other-directed. Your children need to see this in the way you deal with your family and friends. And you need to explain it.

We really enjoy social occasions—parties, cookouts, sports, trips, games—because of the *people*, not the activities themselves. We have the most fun when we make our friends happy. In a sense, leisure activities are a reason, almost an excuse, to enjoy our friends' company.

For instance, we generally do not say to friends, "Let's sit down and converse." We say, "Let's have a cup of coffee, or a drink." The beverage itself is unimportant; what counts is the time spent together sharing a few laughs with a friend. When a husband and wife share a drink before dinner, what counts is the sharing, not the drink.

You should go out of your way to have friends over to your house. Your children will learn a lot. They will learn, through their eyes, how to be a good host—that is, how we exert ourselves to please our friends. They will see how good friendship preserves for us, all our lives, some of the joys and laughter we knew in childhood. Warm friendship keeps us young in spirit, no matter what our age.

Children will also learn, especially if you explain it, how real friendship is based on respect. Good friends deeply respect each other and are proud of each other. (A "friendship" without this respect is just familiarity, and familiarity breeds contempt.) Friends do not share just amusements. They share their confidence in each other. They share their hearts.

One subtle result of entertaining friends at home is that your children see other adults respect *you*. Your friends' obvious esteem for you enhances your children's pride in you. This goes a long way to enhance your effectiveness as a parent.

★ ★ ★

In sum then, your task in teaching all these virtues is to build healthy confidence in your children.

Confidence comes from knowing the *truth* about ourselves. We know our shortcomings, our strengths, and our potential strengths—and we know these truths from our experience with life. We know, moreover, that God gives his all-powerful help when we need it to surpass our limitations. "The Lord is my light and my salvation; whom should I fear? The Lord is my life's refuge; of whom should I be afraid?" (Psalm 27: 1,2).

Confidence comes from *love*. Children surrounded by strong, sacrificial family love grow up to be self-confident men and women. Love strengthens everything good in our lives. Love makes anything possible. Love leads us to dare. Love turns life into a great adventure.

7

Love for Jesus Christ

LOVE IS THE LIFELINE that will save your children. God's love for your family, your love for him and your spouse and children, your children's love for family and God—this thread of unified love will course down the years through your children's destiny. With the help of God, it will direct them to live honorably, to turn their hearts ever toward God, and to win eternal life.

It is your life's divine mission to impart in your children a love for God that will last them all their lives.

God gave you each of your beloved children for one reason: that you labor in family life to lead each of them back to him—now, and later, and forever. He will hold you to account for how well you do this. It is your greatest responsibility.

Reflect on this whenever you tiptoe into your children's bedrooms at night and look down upon them sleeping: In the future, at that moment in time when they finally close their eyes in death, will they be as much in friendship with God as they are right now? Having lived to please God all their lives, as they learned in childhood, will they finally gaze on his face and receive his loving embrace forever?

This thought should drive you on, impel you to surpass yourself, strengthen you through any adversity. God calls you to live like a saint, to achieve the heights of holiness, by leading your children to virtue and everlasting life.

Your children's religious upbringing cannot be done in fits and starts, with mere superficial acts of piety inserted into family life. Your family's religious practice must not be something "extra," something helpful but unessential. It cannot be a protective garment put on in troubled times and then later put away like a raincoat or umbrella.

If your children adopt this misguided attitude, seeing faith-life as a bunch of shallow habitual practices, they may (probably will) leave religion behind them. As they grow, they may abandon God and his Church along with their toys and dolls and Santa Claus. This, as we have seen, could lead to tragedy.

Only a deep, heartfelt personal love for God—God loved through and through in the family, God dwelling alive in the hearts of one's parents—will last your children a lifetime and direct their lives aright.

What does this vocational mission mean for you?

It means you must struggle *to know God personally,* to see him vividly as he is: a person with mind and heart and will, an all-powerful loving Father, the greatest of all friends, the one Friend who will never let you and your family down. Your children will not really know God this way if their vision is confined to plaster statues and stained glass images. They will know him most deeply from what you teach them with your life. They will come to share your vision of him—a real, living, loving Person—or they will have no vision at all.

You must struggle *to love God personally,* to love him with the same affection you extend to the other great loves in your life. You begin this by grasping that breathtaking central fact of our faith: that God loves each of us infinitely—with far greater passion, tenderness, and devotional sacrifice than the greatest love a mother can have for her child. Here on earth, any of us can withstand anything if we know that someone somewhere is crazy about us, loves us absolutely no matter what. The driving force of Christian life, the secret of every saint's holiness, is to know that God loves each of us this way, and he longs for us to love him back.

Love leads to service. And so you must strive *to serve God personally,* right where he has placed you, among your family and friends and all those other people (strangers to you now) whose lives God has arranged to intersect with your own. You serve him by serving them. You take the powers he has given you and direct them toward others' needs. Some people in your life need help and encouragement, and this you extend through your friendship. Some are burdened down with a life of pointless drudgery, and you teach them, by your life's example, the Christian secret of happiness. Everyone needs to find God. Your friends will find him in your confident eyes, your heartfelt words, your deeds of service. This is your apostolate.

Your children, too, will fall in love with Jesus Christ for life when they encounter him in you: in your eyes, your words, the way you serve him in the countless details of family life. Christ will be real to them when he is alive in your heart.

The face of Jesus

This *personal* dimension of your love for God cannot be overemphasized. You must know and love Christ personally if you are to lead your children to him. Your children cannot really love and serve a faceless abstraction.

You must lead your children, therefore, to picture the face of Jesus: his holy humanity the way it was and is, the expression in his eyes when he turns his face to us, the countenance we envision when we pray to him, the face that will greet us joyfully at the moment of death.

Hear the words that Pope John Paul II addressed to young people, including you and your children . . .

"Jesus is not an idea, a sentiment, a memory! Jesus is a 'person,' always alive and present with us!"

"This is what education is all about, this is the meaning of life: to know Christ."

". . . The most beautiful and stirring adventure that can happen to you is the personal meeting with Jesus. . . ."

"It is my hope that . . . you will experience what the Gospel means when it says: *'Jesus, looking upon him, loved him'* (Matthew 10: 21). May you experience a look like that! May you experience the truth that he, Christ, looks upon you with love!"

As our Holy Father suggests, the place where we encounter Jesus is in the Gospels. Christ comes alive to us personally when we read the Scriptures. In the accounts of the evangelists, we see Jesus as others saw him. We see his face.

You may have made some resolutions so far while reading this book, some practices to make part of your parental life. One of the most vital, one that will give vigor to the others, is *to read the New Testament every day,* even for just a few minutes.

You should read it slowly and carefully, like a love letter, for that is what it really is. Every phrase of narrative, every word from the mouth of Jesus, every description of Christ's dealings with those around him, the reactions he provoked in people—all these nuanced details will make Christ appear alive to you, someone as personally present to you as your spouse and children. This has been the collective experience of the Church for two thousand years.

If you have a daily custom of reading the Gospel, your children will notice. Your older children, if you encourage them, can be led to do the same; they can continue the custom for life, or return to it later—and it can save them.

Once we seek Jesus, we find him. If we look on his face in childhood, if we loved him once with the pure love of a child, we remember the encounter for life. The eyes of Christ remain in our heartfelt memory. When we look at the tabernacle, we see his face looking back, the face we first met in the Gospels.

Like many other Catholics, you may find it easier to picture Christ's face by looking at the photographs of modern saints. Since the invention of photography, we can now see how saints looked in real life. Because they identified with Jesus wholeheartedly, their countenances resemble his own. Especially in the eyes, the window of the soul.

Look at the photographs of Don Bosco, Therese of Lisieux, Pope Pius X, Maximilian Kolbe, Blessed Miguel Pro, Blessed Josemaria Escriva, and other holy people of the past century, including some still living today. Though quite different in temperament, they all have remarkably similar eyes. They all have a certain look in common. Surely it is not too much to say that their eyes resemble those of Christ, their countenance is his own. What we see in their faces is what the disciples saw when Jesus walked among them.

What do we see in the eyes of a saint? What was in the eyes of Jesus that impressed everyone who saw him?

We see passionate love. The eyes of Jesus and the saints are those of people deeply in love. We see such a look in the eyes of mothers and fathers cuddling their newborn child, betrothed couples glancing at each other, warm friends meeting after a long separation, small children smiling up at their parents.

We see serenity and deep happiness, for love brings inner peace and a confident joy that nothing can shake. All saints live on top of life, and their countenances show it.

We see traces of suffering, too, for love means sacrificial self-denial. But suffering gives way to happiness and indeed engenders it.

We see good humor, the lightness of heart that children know, a readiness for laughter. In the eyes of the saints, we even see a kind of mischievous mirth—as though they were silently sharing some cosmic inside joke with God: that his presence in the soul turns life into a grand, comic adventure.

How often do we think of Jesus laughing, his face radiant with good humor? Yet he must have been like this. Humor is one of the traits we admire most in people, and he had all perfections. As far as we know, all the saints in history enjoyed good humor; some like Philip Neri and Thomas More were famous for it. Surely Christ, the model for them all and the source of their happiness, must have had dazzling good

humor. When his disciples gathered around him, enjoying his
company (as we know they did), surely the most common
sound among them was good-natured laughter.

So then, this is the face of Jesus as you should see it: full
of passionate love, deep happiness, serenity through suffering,
and warm good humor. If you picture Jesus like this before
you, looking at you and your family, your stories about him
to your children will come alive.

As we saw earlier in this book, your children love stories, and you should tell them all sorts of stories to direct
their lives. The Gospels have the greatest stories of all for
children. When you have read the evangelists' accounts
deeply, when you have come to know Jesus intimately
through their pages, you can lead your children to know and
love him as you do.

You can relate the wonderful story of our salvation . . .
how Jesus looked and acted, the things he said and did, the
way he loved and served everyone, his love for us in the
sacraments he founded, the loneliness and horror of his Passion, how he left us his Church as a family, how he remains
with us forever in the Eucharist.

One of the most beautiful traits of children (at their best)
is their capacity for mercy, the tender pity they extend to the
afflicted. They care for wounded little animals. They are moved
by others' tears. They feel sorry for people treated unjustly.

Compassion is often the beginning of love. In leading
your children through the Gospels, you can direct their pure
hearts to have compassion for Jesus, the first stirrings of their
lifelong love for him.

Lead your children to see Jesus' face when he suffered
disappointment. How did Christ look upon the rich young

man who rejected his call and selfishly walked away? After he explained the Eucharist to his disciples (John 6), many of them abandoned him; he turned to his apostles and asked, "Will you also go away?" What was the look on his face? When he handed Judas a morsel of food at the Last Supper, a final gesture of affection, what look did he give his betrayer? And after Peter denied him, St. Luke says (22: 61–62), "the Lord turned and looked upon Peter . . . and Peter went out and wept bitterly." What was in that look of Jesus? How does he look on us when *we* deny him?

Help your children also to see Jesus moved with compassion. How did he look upon the lepers who cried desperately for his help? Or the heartbroken parents begging a cure for their children? Or the tears in his eyes as he approached the grave of Lazarus, and when he wept over unrepentant Jerusalem?

How his face must have shone, deeply moved, to see a poor widow give God her last coin, all she had to live on (Mark 12: 41–44)—for to be "poor in spirit" is to put *all* our trust in God.

Picture the scene with Bartimeus the blind man, who shouted to Jesus for help and would not be silenced by the crowds (Mark 10: 46-52). Christ called to him and asked what he wanted, and Bartimeus replied, "Lord, that I may see!" Instantly, Jesus gave him sight.

Think of this blind man's first experience with sight. His lifelong blackness tore aside like a veil, and his eyes beheld for the first time shape, movement, color. The very first image he ever saw was the face of Jesus looking straight into his eyes. What did Jesus look like? At that dazzling moment, what did Bartimeus see in the eyes and smile of his Savior?

If you can picture that same face looking into yours, your heart will be moved to pray.

Lead your children to see how, in so many different ways, Jesus said *Trust me.* . . . He spoke of "birds of the air" and "lilies of the field" to explain God's love for us, how he provides for us like a good Father. He said over and again that all we must do is repent and ask, and God will take care of our needs. For those who love God, as St. Paul said, everything works out for the good.

And of course, you should lead your children to pity Jesus in his sacred Passion. It was caused by sin, including every sin of ours. He suffered to free us from sin, to save us from hell's everlasting sorrow.

Your children should form a vivid image of the Passion, one that will fix in their minds and consciences for life. Help them to feel sorrow for Jesus, and thereby sorrow for their sins. . . . Christ was betrayed by one of his chosen apostles, a man who had seen his miracles and heard his teachings but who was blinded by pride and greed. In the garden, he cried and sobbed, heartbroken, weighed down with the sins of the world. His friends abandoned him, left him alone. He was arrested and hauled before a court, assaulted by lies and unjust accusation. He was punched, spat upon, stripped of his clothing, beaten almost to death with iron-tipped whips, crowned with thorns so that his face was smeared with blood. Mobs of people yelled at him, called him vile names as he carried his cross. Spikes were driven through his hands and feet, and he hung from his wounds on the cross until he died in agony. The only loved ones by his side were his mother, St. John, and some valiant women.

Teach your children: Jesus did this to save each of us, every single person by name, including everyone in your family. Since God is above time, every one of our sins assaults him in his Passion. Every time we offend God, we act like the people who attacked him. But he showed mercy to one of those arresting him, curing his wounded ear. He forgave those who crucified him. He forgave a repentant thief who died with him. And he forgives us if we are sorry for our sins and apologize to him in confession.

All these vivid personal stories of Christ should lead your children to see his compassionate face before them, now and for the rest of their lives. Once they learn to love him, they will never forget him. When faced with strong temptations to sin later in life, in adolescence and adulthood, what can pull them back, lead them to resist, and save them will be two vivid memories—the pure love for Christ they learned as children, and your loving voice, the voice of their conscience, directing them toward heaven.

There is one final Gospel incident we can look at here, a scene that should hit home to you as a parent and give you hope. . . .

Mothers were pressing forward to Jesus with their children, hoping he would lay his hands on them and bless them. When his disciples tried to hold them back, Jesus sharply told them to stop, to let the mothers and children through to him.

How did Jesus look at these valiant women? With affection and gratitude certainly; but perhaps also with some amusement, for surely his disciples had their hands full trying to turn back a group of determined mothers. These women, like all valiant Christian parents since, would let

nothing and no one deter them from leading their children
to their Savior.

Personal prayer

You will also show Christ to your children if you seek
him in personal prayer.

This is not vocal prayer, words we speak aloud or read
from some text. It is rather the silent inner prayer of Christians who seek to converse intimately with Jesus.

Briefly put, it is to set aside a brief time—15 to 30 minutes or whatever we can manage—and speak inwardly with
God, talking to him and listening, getting to know him better and bringing our innermost concerns to him. It is like sitting down for a while with a warm friend and chatting about
everyday things. It is to spend time in the presence of One
we love.

Where to do this? The best place, of course, is in front of
the tabernacle. This is why we reserve the Eucharist outside
of Mass, so we can adore God and speak with him.

But we can also pray anywhere else free from distrac-
tions, even in a room at home. Our Lord even described this:
"But when you pray, go into your room, and closing the
door, pray to your Father in secret; and your Father, who sees
in secret, will reward you" (Matthew 6: 6).

Where can you, a busy parent, find the time? The answer
is that, if you want to do anything important, you somehow
find the time. All of us *make* time for whatever we value
highly, no matter how busy we are. You know this from your
own experience. Even busy parents make time for chatting
on the phone with friends, reading the sports page, getting

regular exercise, puttering in the garden, whatever enriches life in some small but significant way.

It is really a question of priorities. What comes ahead of what? Where is our heart?

Imagine it this way. Many parents send their children off to college and then wait for a letter or phone call. They wait and wait. . . . The longer they wait, the more hurt they feel, and justly. If their grown son or daughter does not write in the first couple of weeks, this is surely understandable; a great many new activities crowd out the time to write. But if their child fails to write over a three-month period, this is hurtful and even insulting. It really means that every single thing their child did in that time, no matter how trivial, was more important than writing Mom and Dad. Sending a letter home took absolutely last place in their child's priorities.

Silence is sometimes a snub. And it hurts.

You, as a parent, can well identify with this situation. If one of your children treated you this way, ignoring you, declining to write or call, you would be deeply hurt. You could then imagine Christ's poignant words to Peter and the others in the Garden of Gethsemane as he faced his Passion alone: "Could you not, then, watch one hour with me?" (Matthew 26: 41).

He asks all Christians, including you, the same question: Can't you spend some time with me? Even a little? Don't you realize how much I want to hear from you, be with you? Why do you ignore me?

Setting aside 20 minutes a day to converse with God is the least we can do. It pleases Jesus, and he deserves it—like parents hearing often from beloved children who have moved away.

Personal prayer is, in a sense, natural to a Christian, something to be expected in any warm friendship, which is how we should deal with our Savior. This is why so many thousands of Christian parents today make the time for daily mental prayer.

How do busy parents go about this? They put the time in their schedule and do their best to stick with it; this is half the struggle. They take a copy of the Gospels or some spiritual book with them to the place they find most suitable, some quiet part of the house away from a phone. They begin with a short vocal prayer such as the "Hail Mary," asking Our Lady's help to talk with Jesus as naturally as she did in Nazareth. Then they begin to converse with God, talking about anything—for he is interested in whatever concerns us.

You can talk with him about your family, each member of it one by one. Express your concerns, your hopes . . . ask his advice what to do . . . leave your worries in his powerful hands.

You can glance through the Gospels, too, trying to know him better, to see some lesson or insight in his words that escaped you before. You read a few lines, a couple of paragraphs, then set the book down and reflect; talk things over with him. Sometimes, when you put a problem before him, you will open the Gospel to a passage that answers you perfectly. God answers you not only with some inner voice but also with what you read in prayer.

You may sometimes take another spiritual work and use it the same way. The Old Testament is full of stirring, inspiring holy passages, especially in Isaiah and the Psalms. The Psalms display passionate love for God and confidence in his merciful power. So many of the Psalms hit home poignantly to parents.

David, like any Christian father and mother, felt the burden of responsibility and turned confidently to God for help.

You may also find food for your prayer in *The Imitation of Christ,* one of the great works of Christian spirituality. Though written mainly for consecrated religious, it is valuable as well for lay people.

Since you are a lay person, a busy parent in the middle of the world, you may find what you want in the works of Blessed Josemaria Escriva, the holy founder of Opus Dei. He labored under God's inspiration to teach lay men and women, single and married and in all occupations, to find Christ and serve him in the midst of normal daily life. Several of his works—*The Way, The Forge, Furrow, Way of the Cross*—were written specifically to help lay people, including parents, in daily mental prayer. Look through these works and see for yourself.

Consider, for instance, what Blessed Josemaria Escriva said about personal mental prayer:

"You don't know how to pray? Put yourself in the presence of God, and as soon as you have said, 'Lord, I don't know how to pray!' you can be sure you've already begun" (*The Way,* #90).

"You wrote to me: 'To pray is to talk with God. But about what?' About what? About him, and yourself: joys, sorrows, successes and failures, great ambitions, daily worries— even your weaknesses! And acts of thanksgiving and petitions—and love and reparation. . . . In short, to get to know him and to get to know yourself—to get acquainted!" (*The Way,* #91).

To pray like this is so easy, so simple in form and execution, that one wonders why so few Christian parents do it.

Personal prayer gives enormous strength to daily family life. God comes to dwell in the hearts of the parents and thus enters, mysteriously, into the hearts of their children. A parent who prays is confident, never alone, never without hope. Christ is always right there in family life, just within reach.

If you pray this way, of course, your children will ask about it. What are you up to? You can explain you are praying for each of them, one by one. And you can ask each to do the same for you. Your older children especially can learn to follow your example, and this habit of daily life can last through adolescence, through all of life. If they see what a difference prayer makes in you, they will seek to follow you. They will be men and women of prayer.

What better gift can you give your children than a lifelong intimacy with Jesus Christ?

The Eucharist

If the Eucharistic Sacrifice is the center of your life, it will change the lives of your children. No prayer is greater, none more powerful, than the Mass, for it was devised by Christ himself—whose words comprise its essential prayers, and who is both priest and sacrificial victim on the altar.

To live the Mass well is to lift up, together with Christ, our heart and mind and will to God the Father. It is to offer him all the details of our daily life with the bread and wine. It is to relive the bloody sacrifice of Calvary, the way to our eternal life. It is to consume him wholly in Communion, receiving him as food and life within us. It is to become one with him who became one of us, and remains with us forever.

If you really live the Mass this way, in your attitude and affections, your reverence and participation, it will be part of your children's lives as long as they live. At some later time in their lives, in adolescence or young adulthood—and especially when they begin their families—they will grow to see the Mass as a priceless family heirloom: a treasure passed on with sacrificial loyalty through generations of forebears to them and their children. The Mass, they will understand, has been part of their family's life for centuries, as life-giving as the family's common blood.

Your children will see it this way, that is, if you explain it to them. At the onset of adolescence, children grow to understand how they are the latest in a family line extending back through history. Their blood, their facial features, their family name and customs have coursed through a line of parents and children down to them. Love for the Eucharistic Sacrifice has lived at the core of this family lineage, a thread binding parents and children to each other and to God.

You can explain this beautiful heritage to your children if you understand it yourself and if they see how much it means to you. You can explain it like this . . .

The Eucharistic Sacrifice was established by Christ and has threaded its way through Christian history, generation after generation. At some point in your family's lineage, more than a thousand years ago, your forebears bent their heads to receive the waters of Baptism and made the Mass central to their lives, the focus of their gratitude to God. This loyalty to our central Christian worship passed from parents to children, parents to children, down the centuries, often at great personal sacrifice. In our time, at the turn of the 21st century, it has come to you and your family. Your children, please God, will embrace it as their lifeline—binding them to you and Christ—and will pass it on to your grandchildren.

Teach this to your children. Show them your hope that they will grow in that love, nurture it in the decades of life to come, never part from it no matter what.

You teach this, as with all your other life-lessons, through your example.

Dress well for the Mass, and lead your children to do the same. If we dress well for guests, we should dress well for Christ. He is our greatest Guest, more worthy of honor than anyone.

Remember that your children watch you during Mass, when you take no notice of their glances. They can read everything in your eyes. They can tell if you are attentive or bored, prayerful or distracted, happy to be there or wishing that the priest would hurry up and finish. Are your eyes on the altar, or do you glare at your wristwatch? Children have eyes for attitude, and they miss nothing.

So let your children see your comportment during Mass: your attention to what is taking place, your voice raised in prayer and song, your silent prayers (for them) in the offertory, your reverence to the Sacred Host elevated at the consecration, your prayerful welcome to him at Communion. Your posture at Mass, your gestures of heartfelt worship, the very look on your face—all of this will convey to your children how much the Mass means to you. This they will remember.

They will remember all the more vividly if you attend Mass and receive the Eucharist during the week. This custom involves sacrifice; it can complicate family life a bit. But in a broader sense, it simplifies that life as well. It puts matters in priority: God first, every day. The grace of Christ in daily communion gives greater peace in the house, more patience among everyone, deeper growth in the children's character. There is something special, something spiritually attractive in children whose parents receive Christ each day.

Tell your children that you pray for them during Mass. When bread and wine are offered to God, you offer your daily work for the family. When Christ appears miraculously on the altar, you beg him to watch over your family. When you receive him, you give heartfelt thanks for all his gifts and blessings for your family, most of all for the gift of himself within all of you. Let your children know how you put your family into the Mass, and this is why God lives in the family's heart.

Someday years ahead, when your grown sons and daughters take their children to Mass, they will remember what you taught them in childhood. They will pray for their children as you prayed for them.

Never speak badly of a priest, ever. No matter what his personal shortcomings (and we all have them), he has a sacred mission intertwined with your own. He has given up wife and children to serve our common family, the Church; so your family is part of his own. At the moment of his ordination, he received the powers of Christ conferred on the apostles and passed down through generations of bishops: the divine powers to forgive sins and to turn bread and wine into Christ.

This is your priest's mission, to give Christ's life to your family. You should lead your children, then, to give every priest their affectionate respect, gratitude, and loyalty. Lead your children to pray for the priest, especially during the Eucharistic Sacrifice. If priests today have problems, it is because we do not pray enough for them.

You should be aware, as well, of the great influence your family can have on a priest. Any dedicated priest will tell you: Seeing a truly pious family receive Communion greatly strengthens a priest's vocation and gives him hope for the Church. In well-formed children, alive to God through their parents' sacrifices, a priest sees Christ himself.

A virtuous family alive to Christ gives glory to God.

8

Deeds

A LOVE WITHOUT DEEDS is scarcely love at all. We expect love to show itself in action, in what love leads us to do. You show your love for God to your children in what you do for him, and what you lead them to do—by your example, directed practice, and word.

To use a comparison that Christ himself used: the faith of parents is like salt in family life. Christians are to be the salt of the world; in their loving deeds of faith, Christian parents are the salt of their family. What does this mean?

Salt gives greater flavor to everything it seasons. Christian spirituality brings virtue, peace, and joy to every aspect of family life.

Even amidst the normal squabbles and hassles of family life, a Christian family is profoundly happy, a joy to grow up in. Salt saves from corruption. Christian devotion preserves married love and saves family members from the death of sin.

Salt works best when it permeates food entirely. Acts of loving faith course naturally through everything in family life. A few important acts done conscientiously and well affect family life from within.

So when we speak of devotions, we do not mean a large number of clustered activities. Numbers do not count. Christ disapproved, we recall, of multiplying prayers for the sake of mere augmenting. It is spirit that matters, a fundamental attitude shown in just a few crucial areas. If these few deeds are done sincerely out of love, they profoundly affect children's religious upbringing.

Here they are. . . .

Visits

We Catholics claim that inside each tabernacle rests Jesus Christ, God and perfect man, the all-powerful Maker of the universe who sustains us in existence and protects us from evil, the Holy One to whom all believing parents entrust their children's protection.

And yet during the days of the week, our churches lie empty. One or two elderly or homeless people may drop in for a time, but the benches lie bare. In front, the tabernacle sits as if waiting for someone, but no one's eyes see it. The Lord of the Universe waits alone, his only company a little flame flickering in the shadows.

No wonder people outside our faith have doubts about our sincerity of belief. They have a point. If we Catholics sincerely believe in the Real Presence, why do we stay away from him? If we truly loved him as God and friend, why do we find it so burdensome, such a hassle, to pay the Blessed Sacrament some adoration during the week? Or even the simple courtesy of a friendly visit? Some faith!

Faith is largely a matter of priorities. Where does the love of God come in our lives? What comes ahead of it?

The early Christian martyrs suffered death rather than live a lie. They loved God too much to deny him by offering worship to a creature. A pinch of incense made the difference between life and death. But to them God came first in love, then everything else most dear—family, friends, work, leisure, laughter, all the good delights of life they left behind.

What do so many Catholics put ahead of visiting the Blessed Sacrament, spending just a few moments in prayer? To visit him is just as easy as dropping clothes at the cleaners, or getting the car washed, or stopping to fill a tank of gas. No more time involved; no more effort. Indeed visiting Our Lord in the tabernacle is easier, less time consuming than walking the dog or jogging a couple of miles. Why is this custom, then, at the bottom of people's priorities, or even wholly unconsidered from one day to the next?

There is no ill feeling toward God here, surely. No smoldering grudge or resentment. No offense intended. What is it then? Indifference?

But indifference is a deeply hurtful thing in any close relationship. You, as a parent, should know this.

When all is said and done, indifference and ingratitude, not hate, are the cruelest opposites of love. A family marked by children's thankless indifference is a sad place. Shakespeare said it through King Lear: "How sharper than a serpent's tooth it is to have a thankless child!"

After all his suffering, Jesus is met with our thankless indifference. We would rather do nearly anything, it seems, than spend a few minutes in his company. A matter of priorities.

There is little you can do to bring crowds to visit the Blessed Sacrament, but you can visit him yourself and take along your children.

This one custom in your family life, to visit God with your children for just a few minutes—to drop by to see a Friend, to chat in prayer for a moment—can deeply affect your children's faith and their lifetime love for God.

It will, for one thing, show them you mean it: that your family's love for God comes first in your life. And you hope it will be first in theirs.

You teach your sincere priorities.

You can lead them to express gratitude to Christ—thanks for all his blessings, for giving you each other in the family, for giving all of us eternal life, for giving us himself in the tabernacle. When someone sends us a gift, we drop by to express our gratitude. It is right and fair to do this and rude to fail in it. Only spoiled children, of any age, would answer a favor with indifference. Teach this to your children.

You can also appeal to their pity for Christ, which can deepen their love for him: "See how alone he is. No one else is here. How lonely he must feel just waiting for some friend to drop by, someone who cares about him and just wants to talk a while. Let's pray to him just for a minute. It must mean a lot to him. . . ."

If you direct your children's pure hearts to the tabernacle, their love will enter within and remain there. All their lives, no matter what may befall them, they will remember.

This is important for you to remember. Your children may later forget many details of the faith you teach them. They may struggle to remember words of childhood prayers or answers to questions of the catechism. But they will remember this: Your faith was *important* to you.

Someday years hence, one of your children may suffer some crisis in life, some crushing, heartbreaking burden. He may have drifted from the faith, willfully or through indifference, and have nowhere to turn. Walking through a city's streets in the depths of distress, he may come upon a church, pause, and feel somehow a pull to enter within.

Stepping into the quiet, glancing at the tabernacle ahead, he would feel a rush of memories evoked by his surroundings: the cool trickle of holy water on the forehead, the faint smell of candles and incense, bright splashes of color from stained glass, the candle burning before the tabernacle. It would all come back to him, visiting Jesus with his parents so long ago, praying to God as a child, the happiness he knew then when he lived innocently in the state of grace.

These memories of innocence, and what was important to you, could lead him to confession, and a new beginning.

Never forget this principle, a truth that Christian parents have experienced so many times: When we try to do something in loving service to God, we always underestimate the good God draws out of it.

Reconciliation

Someone once asked G. K. Chesterton why he became a Catholic. He did not launch into a long reasoned explanation. He said simply, "Because I wanted my sins forgiven."

Christ gave each of his priests his power to forgive sins. A priest probes our conscience and judges our repentance in the name of Christ. Then, in the name of Christ and with Christ's authority, he pronounces the words of forgiveness, "I absolve you from your sins. . . ."

On only two occasions does a priest speak and act directly as Christ, using the pronoun "I." One is during the

Mass: "This is *my* Body . . . This is *my* Blood . . . Do this in memory of *me*." The other is during the sacrament of Reconciliation: "*I* absolve you. . . ."

Once your children are old enough, you should take them regularly to confession. Jesus waits for them there, as he waits for you. He wants you to prepare the children for his forgiveness; you do this by helping them form their consciences, teaching them right from wrong.

You may not probe into their consciences, of course— only Christ and his priest may do this—but you do teach the standards of right conduct, explaining to them which thoughts and actions of ours offend God and therefore call for sacramental apology.

This teaching, as you can see, relates directly to your family life: rightful and loving authority, clear standards of justice and charity, insistence on apology where this is called for, forgiveness and a new beginning.

If your children see you confess your sins regularly, they will see you living Christian responsibility: the truth that we are always children of God, no matter what our age, and we answer to him all our lives. He is always our loving Father. No matter how old we are, we never outgrow the need for his forgiveness.

Christ said to all of us, "Let the little children come to me, and do not hinder them, for of such is the kingdom of God. Amen I say to you, whoever does not accept the kingdom of God as a little child will not enter into it" (Luke 18: 16-17).

Little children are simple and sincere, trusting, innocent and pure of heart. This is what each of us must be to win heaven. And this is what the sacrament of Reconciliation does for us. It restores us to childlike innocence. When we sincerely and humbly confess our sins, Christ forgives us, washes us clean of guilt. His reward for our apology is to give us once again the purity and innocence, the happiness and peace of mind, the sheer delight in being alive that we knew as tiny children.

This is a knowledge your children need for life: Confession restores us to the joy of childhood.

One final point, a warning implicit in Christ's words above: Parents who fail to lead their children to Christ— who "hinder" them through exampled religious neglect, especially of this sacrament—will answer to God for it.

Charity and justice

Thoughts of Christ's love and forgiveness in confession lead us to consider living charity and justice in the home.

If your mouth opens in prayer one moment and then later speaks badly of someone, your children will come to see you as a hypocrite. The epistles of Paul and James contain blistering condemnations of uncharitable speech among Christians. St. James says, " . . .the tongue is a fire, the very world of iniquity" (James 3: 6).

Strive to keep gossip, scandal-mongering, and rash judgment out of your family, and begin with yourself. Insist on this among your children. Backbiting gossip poisons a family's spirit; it stains people's hearts. So teach your children this: If we cannot say something positive about people, we say nothing.

This is not just a matter of charity. It is justice as well. We have no right to judge others badly, or to meddle (even with talk) in their private matters, or to attack them when they cannot defend themselves. To do any of these things is unjust. It offends God, and we will not offend him or others.

What about scandalous behavior from political and media figures? Lead your children to distinguish between the fault and the person. We "hate the sin, but love the sinner." We deplore what people do, but we bear them no personal ill will, and we pray for them. We may work to oust our pro-abortion senator from office, but we pray for his soul. We may refuse to watch some popular entertainer's TV show, but we pray she will someday join us in heaven.

Your children must learn that charity does not mean just giving away old clothes. It means mostly compassionate understanding.

Catechism

St. Paul said, "I will pray with the spirit, but I will pray with the understanding also" (I Corinthians 14: 15).

Our religion is not merely a collection of binding activities nor an emotional stance of the soul. Faith is ultimately truth, and we grasp truth with our mind.

Religious upbringing, therefore, means to grow in understanding the truths of human existence—who God is, who we are, where we are headed, what we must do and avoid in this life to win life eternal.

We find these truths in our catechism.

Our Catholic catechism is not just a set of topics to study and memorize. It is not merely a course to complete before sacramental Confirmation and then put aside for good. It is something for us to learn and accept thoroughly, *all of it, without exceptions.*

In his final words to his apostles, Christ said: "Go, therefore, and make disciples of all nations, . . . teaching them to observe *all* that I have commanded you. . . ." (Matthew 28: 19-20). Down through the ages, our Church has done just this, taught *everything* that Christ taught, *all* that he commanded. In one age or another, some of Christ's teachings have been unpopular, some of his Church's doctrines have met with opposition. We see this today with his teachings about marriage, contraception, sexual morality. Regardless of "public opinion" or people's desire to believe selectively (so to speak), the Church has been faithful to Christ's clear command.

It is a curious thing, in fact, how picking and choosing what to believe leads eventually to a tattering of one's faith.

If we refuse to accept a single serious Church teaching (say, contraception), we are implicitly denying the authority of the Church to teach at all. If the Pope and bishops are "wrong" in one area, if what they teach is untrue, then why should we believe any of the rest of it? Indeed, how can we? A serious "error" in one teaching casts doubt on all the rest, on the whole notion of infallibility itself. To tear one thread out of the tapestry is to unravel the whole fabric.

Christ said to Peter and the other apostles, "he who hears you, hears me" (Luke 10: 16). This bold declaration cannot be only partly true, or true only for matters we are pleased with. Either it is true entirely or it is wholly false. A sincere belief in the Church's divine origin and authority leads inexorably to belief in everything it teaches in Christ's name.

Our catechism, then, is an intelligent, systematic explanation of *everything* Christ taught us, both in the Scriptures and through his immortal Mystical Body, the Church. It is the truth about human existence and destiny.

To study it in depth could take a lifetime; indeed the older we are, the more we see and appreciate its aptness and beauty. The catechism is as necessary for adults as it is for children.

You should, therefore, take serious interest in your children's catechetical instruction, to the point of sacrifice if necessary. No study of theirs is more important to them or to you. Literally, the destiny of their souls depends on it.

Taking a serious interest means, among other things, studying the catechism along with your children. It means reading along with them, looking over their shoulders, and answering their questions. It means *you* teach them as you go along. Though you may *delegate* some instruction to teachers in CCD or school, you do not *relegate* it.

People outside the family may support your efforts, but not substitute for them. Most really important lessons are learned at home, from one's parents, or they are not learned at all.

Treat this responsibility, then, like all your other vital family duties. Look at this this way. Though your children sometimes eat outside the family, as in school, it is you who provide most of your children's nutrition. And of course, one way or another you oversee what your children are fed elsewhere. The catechism is food for your children's spiritual life, so most of that nourishment should come from you.

Are you concerned about being up for the job? How can you teach anything that you know so little about? Your hesitation here is understandable.

It is possible, even likely, that your own Catholic instruction as a child was spotty and even entirely misleading. The years following Vatican II were a time of confusion and sloppy catechetics. (Nothing new in this; such a period has surrounded nearly all great Church councils.)

As you look through a sound catechism now, you may notice with dismay huge gaps in your understanding. You may have the impression, quite rightly, that you know little more than your uninstructed children.

This should not concern you. There is a maxim among professional teachers: The best way to learn something is to teach it. We learn something best when we are teaching it to others.

God has arranged, then, that you learn along with your children. By teaching them, you will learn yourself. Together you will grow in knowledge of his truth.

Today, conditions are changing in the Church for the better. Gradually, in fits and starts here and there, we are pulling out of the confusion. Many signs of this can be seen around us. One of the most significant is our new comprehensive catechism. Your family should own a copy, for it is vitally important.

This recently published *Catechism of the Catholic Church* is the first fully comprehensive explanation of Catholic doctrine and morals in four hundred years. It has everything. It was intended as a template for other catechetical works; so, books for children should be based on it, and explicitly so. You should rely only on recent catechisms that refer to it by name and clearly base their text upon its teachings.

When your children receive the sacrament of Confirmation, the Holy Spirit seals them as responsible, "grown-up" Christian adults. At that sacred moment you celebrate in your family, a great gift to your children would be a personal copy of the *Catechism of the Catholic Church*, inscribed appropriately: "From Mom and Dad ... May you live by this faith all your life and pass it on to your children!" This historic work of the Church, a first edition at that, could pass through generations of your children's descendents—along with your family's sacred faith. Is this not what you want?

Teaching your faith directly to your children is, after all, a family tradition. Nearly all your family's forebears learned our Church's faith and prayers from their parents and grandparents. It is a great responsibility for you, indeed an honor, to pass Christ's truth on to your children and grand-children.

When the faith is transmitted this way, personally from parents to children, it is like the passage of lighted candles from hand to hand in our beautiful Easter Vigil liturgy. The fire of Christ's truth, the blaze of his love, lights the way for each family through every generation.

Life and love

Chastity is neither a deprived state of life nor a collection of negative precepts. It is a joyful affirmation, a heart given purely to God in the single state or in marriage.

Marriage is sacred, blessed by God, and its physical act of union is holy.

Sex is all about married love and life, spouse and children; any other use of it thwarts the will of God and gravely offends him.

If we fall into impurity, Christ will reward our repentance and clean us once again through the sacrament of Reconciliation.

Do your growing children understand these principles? Do you direct them to learn about married love and the sacred origins of life? This is one of your greatest responsibilities. It is no exaggeration to say that your patient, affectionate teaching in these matters can determine the course of your children's lives.

In today's society, the forces of materialism—seeing and treating others as objects—relentlessly press upon your children's consciences. Your children are surrounded by an aggressive eroticism, professionally glamorized and presented as "normal." It is the Great Lie: Man is a beast.

Your children will not recognize the Great Lie unless they know the truth. They will not resist its allurements unless you exert yourself to strengthen their consciences and powers of self-control.

If you fail in any of this, you may live to see lamentable, even tragic, consequences in your children's lives: loss of faith, casual promiscuity, shaky or broken marriage, abandonment of children (physical or moral), or refusal to have children at all. If your children enter marriage with a materialistic outlook, their marriages could break apart and you could lose your grandchildren. (The courts care little about the visiting rights of grandparents.) This happens literally every day.

The very thought of these threats should impel you to teach your children the truth about marriage, chaste love, and Christian sexual morality. In this vitally important matter, as with catechetical instruction, you should not abdicate the task to others. It is *your* attitudes that mean everything to your children. No one can adequately substitute for one's parents.

Nor can any "sex ed" course compensate for neglect at home. To be frank about it, the biology of reproduction takes 15 minutes to teach; but the moral aspect, the one that really counts, takes years.

You have years at home to do this, and experienced Christian parents can testify it is easier than we expect. A stronger bond of love, an affectionate respect for one's parents, develops among children whose parents love them enough to teach the truth.

Because this is a complex and delicate area, you need more complete guidance than we can give here. You can begin by reading *The Truth and Meaning of Human Sexuality* published by the Pontifical Council for the Family (1996). Follow its advice. Consult other experienced Christian parents, people who share your principles and whose judgment you respect.

One final matter here. When marriage is highly valued, so also is apostolic celibacy. In any Christian society, a decline of respect for the sanctity of marriage is matched by decline of vocations to celibacy. That is, the vocations are there, for God calls people to serve him in holy dedication one way or another—but people fail to respond.

So, teach your children the meaning of *vocation*. Show them the panorama of their future lives in terms of God's plan for each of them. And be open to accept God's will for them, whatever it turns out to be. If you prepare your children for their life's Providential mission, in holy marriage or holy celibacy, they will hear God's call and, with his grace, answer it.

Prayers

Prayer should be a part of your family life, as natural as family conversation. If God dwells within the family, it is natural for us to include him in family life. If he is included this way, the Holy Spirit fills the family's entire life.

Begin your day with a morning offering, and teach your children to do the same. This is a short prayer of our own composing that we say silently in the early morning. It is a simple thing, but so important.

We thank God for giving us another day of life. We offer everything we will do that day, every thought and word and action, as a sacrificial gift to him. Any Christian who lives this custom finds his daily life changed in subtle ways. The day has more energy, yet more peace. We treat people more kindly and meet setbacks with patience. Our whole day turns into prayer.

Christian families begin meals, too, with a prayer of thanksgiving. We pause to thank God for his sustenance, for his gifts of peace and solidarity in the family, for everything we receive from his hands. A prayer is offered, too, for the homeless and hungry in the world. This beautiful custom binds the family together in prayer at least once a day. Moreover, it has a way of passing down through generations.

Christian parents also lead their children to pray before bedtime. The children thank God for his gift of the day now passing. They ask pardon for anything they did wrong. They ask his protection through the night and the day to come. Saying a simple act of contrition at day's end is a powerful aid to children's consciences. How different their lives (and ours) would be if they continued the custom through adulthood. Nightly "examination of conscience" is an ancient Christian custom, and it leads to frequent, contrite confession.

In a Christian family, too, people are aware of each other's needs and pray for these. People pray, and ask for prayers, in all sorts of tight situations, large and small: illness, upcoming exams in school, interviews for a job, friends and neighbors in special need. Ask your children for their prayers; so few parents do this. The prayers of your children are powerful before God, and he often answers them with startling swiftness.

Lead them to pray also (especially in the rosary) for the Church and the Pope. Our Church, they should understand, is really an extended family. People cannot truly grasp the Church until they see it as a family. Like any other family, like yours, it has a beloved Father. (The word "Pope" is the English form for the Italian "Papa," the affectionate name for a father.) It has a Mother, too, in the Virgin Mary. Like any other family, it has a mission: eternal life for all mankind. It has heroes: the saints. It has anniversaries to celebrate together. It has people separated from the family, and we pray for their return. Like any other family, its members are remarkably different from each other, but everyone is bound together in affectionate unity. What joins us as one in the

Church, as in any family, is God's love for each of us and our love for each other as brothers and sisters.

Any family home contains images of loved ones. And that is why your home should have some images on the walls. (Not too many. Even with family photographs, a display can be overdone.) A crucifix in several rooms (certainly in the children's bedrooms), some pictures of Our Lady, a photograph of the Holy Father—all these are tokens of affection. They remind us of those we love.

9

Our Mother Mary

C hrist gave us our Church as a family, we have seen, and every family needs a mother. So Jesus gave us Mary to be our Blessed Mother forever.

He did this on Calvary when he said to Mary, "Woman, behold your son. . . ," and to John, "Behold your mother" (John 19: 25-27). St. John goes on to relate, "And from that hour the disciple took her into his home."

Catholics have done this ever since, made Mary part of their home.

Mary was and is a woman, and every child needs a woman's touch to grow up right. Every Christian can turn to Mary for the special affection a mother has for her children.

Moreover she is a perfect woman. God made her that way from her conception. How can we understand this? How can you explain it to your children? Maybe like this. . . .

Some of the world's great museums display exquisite chalices as works of art. They are indeed beautiful. Made of the finest gold flawlessly shaped as a cup, they are decorated with priceless diamonds, rubies, emeralds, and other precious stones. All this skillfully crafted beauty goes into each chalice for one reason: it was meant to hold within it the Body and Blood of Jesus Christ, God become perfect man.

For the same reason, God made Mary absolutely perfect. She was to be the Mother of God. She was to hold within her the Body and Blood of God become man. His human nature, all of it, came from her. We are all, therefore, related to Jesus through her.

Once a chalice has held Christ, it ought not to be used for any other drink, not even the finest wine in the world. It was fashioned for only one purpose. Similarly Mary was to remain ever virgin.

Think what we mean when we say she was perfect woman. She was a perfect little girl; she had all the precious qualities you find in your young daughters, with none of the defects. As an adolescent, she had the bright charms of young womanhood. The Holy Spirit was alive in her, she was "full of grace." By her free will, she became the Mother of the Messiah, the Holy One promised to David, her royal forebear, and the prophets of Israel.

She sped swiftly to help her aged cousin Elizabeth, for she is eager to help anyone in need.

As a wife and mother, she filled the household of Nazareth with her feminine care. She did all the tasks any mother anywhere does for her husband and child. The way she did these is a model for every Christian wife and mother.

At the wedding feast of Cana, she first met the disciples of her Son, including young John, who would later take her as mother for us all. We may imagine her gracious hospitality, the warmth with which she greeted these friends of Jesus. During the feast, she noticed—as only a woman would—that the wine had run out, an embarrassment for the newly married couple. For Mary, as for any good woman, there is no such thing as a minor social embarrassment; any important social occasion, especially a wedding, must be perfect. So she pressed Jesus to work an inopportune miracle. He could not refuse her. She said to the servants what she says to us through the centuries: "Do whatever he tells you."

We can learn so much from all this. As we saw earlier, Our Lord worked miracles to prove his divinity and sometimes out of spontaneous compassion. But the singular incident of Cana shows another thing: Jesus will do anything for his Mother, even work a miracle.

Children turn to their mothers when they are in trouble, when some problem bothers them. This is what mothers are for. The problems of children may be tiny in themselves, of little consequence in the great scheme of things, but a mother takes them seriously. What is important to her children is important to her.

So if you have some family problem, some intractable trouble important to you, you can turn to Mary our Mother. She is the specialist, as it were, in small but important problems. You can count on her to intercede with her Son, who can never refuse her no matter what.

Teach this to your children, to have loving confidence in the Mother of God. Have devotion to her as motherly protector of your family.

Say the rosary each day as a family, or some small part of it if your children are very young. As she said at Fatima, it is her favorite prayer. Each "Hail Mary" has the praises given her by Gabriel and Elizabeth, followed by that ancient beautiful prayer of the Church to her:

"Holy Mary, Mother of God, pray for us sinners now and at the hour of our death." Mary should be with your children all their lives and at the moment of death. How can she resist you after you have asked her thousands of times?

The repetition of the rosary's prayers strikes some people as monotonous, and so they shun it. If you are tempted this way, reflect on this: Any great love involves endless repetition.

A mother follows routines day after day, doing the same thing over and over again; this is the way she lovingly serves her family. A father endures a daily commute to and from his workplace and fixed routines throughout his day; this is how he supports his family. Children ask for the same stories every night at bedtime; their parents recount them again and again, overcoming tedium through the delight in their children's eyes. Love means saying, in countless ways, "I love you." That is what our rosary says to the Mother of God.

And besides, as one spiritual author put it, the "monotony" of the rosary matches the shameful monotony of our sins. We keep falling into the same wretched ways, the old familiar ruts of selfishness, with dismaying regularity. We ask our Mother to pull us out, and we ask her over and over again with the rosary. What mother can resist such insistent pleading from children in need?

Another ancient family custom is the May pilgrimage. One appointed day in May, the year's most beautiful month, the whole family briefly visits a shrine to the Blessed Mother and says the rosary together, then celebrates with a picnic. If you make this a family tradition, your children will later look back on it fondly. They will, in a subtle way, associate Mary with the purity and innocence of their childhood. Through God's grace and Our Lady's protection, your grown children could seek that pure innocence again, and find it, through confession.

All this may sound somewhat strange to you, or something you only vaguely remember from childhood. The last quarter of the 20th century has been a materialistic era, and in such times devotion to Mary declines in fashion. (She has enemies, as Jesus does.) But your grandparents and forebears lived a deep devotion to the Blessed Mother. Rosaries were prayed for your family line long before you were born. It is no exaggeration to say that your family is Catholic today because your forebears prayed the rosary.

For your children's sake, return to that piety. Let devotion to Mary mark your family life. The Mother of God will lead your children and grandchildren to her Son.

Queen of the family, pray for us!

10

Confidence

This book has laid out a course of action for you, a great challenge to your faith and inner powers. Every divine mission does this.

Perhaps as you see the task before you—raising your children, one day at a time, to responsible Christian maturity—you may feel daunted, even overwhelmed, at the magnitude of your responsibility. Where will you get the strength?

Take courage. You will receive it from God. He it is who gave you your children and the mission of being his servant for their salvation. You will receive strength from his Blessed Mother, who was faithful to her vocation and who understands the trials of fathers and mothers.

God and Mary will give you courage, wisdom, and perseverance when you most need help. All you need to do is ask, then move into action as best you can. Remember what Christ said to his followers, including you, in so many different ways and words: *Trust me!*

Listen to the promise of God spoken through the words of the prophet Isaiah (49: 15-16): "Can a mother forget her infant, be without tenderness for the child of her womb? Even should she forget, I will never forget you. See, upon the palms of my hands I have written your name; your walls are ever before me."

The walls of your home are ever before the eyes of God. He will never forget you, never let you down. Once you welcome him into your family's heart, he will never leave you. He has promised.

You may understand this clearly for now. In this moment, you may have deep faith and hope in God's all-powerful help, the lifeline he extends to you from day to day. Nonetheless, you know your weaknesses well enough to predict times of darkness ahead, moments when your strength will falter. Like Peter walking on the water, you may feel yourself sinking despite your best efforts and your holy intentions.

At such times, you should do what many other Christian parents do, a practice that never fails to bring peace. . . .

Tiptoe into your children's bedrooms at night when they are sound asleep, and quietly approach their beds.

There they lie before you, your precious gifts from God, your sacred mission in life. As you look down upon them, you sense yourself in the presence of mystery. He, God, is here with you and your children. You sense his presence.

Through the veins of each child flows the blood of forebears past, now gone home to God, who were once children themselves and then grew in turn to look down on their children, as you do now. The line of family love through ages past now lives on, mysteriously, in your children.

Within the soul of each sleeping child, the Holy Spirit lives with all the splendor of baptismal purity. Each of them is, for now, wholly alive to God.

As you look at them, your inner eye casts toward their future. What is God's destiny for them in life? What marvels will they live to see in their allotted span of time? When evil appears before their eyes, as it must, will they have the grace and inner strength to cast it aside? Will their hearts be fixed on the face of Jesus? Will they hear the voice of conscience within, the loving voice of their mother and father, to lead their souls aright?

When you are moved by these thoughts in the presence of your children, you can turn your heart to God in prayer: Merciful God, please give me the strength to change whatever needs changing in me—so I can lead these children of yours, and ours, to become the great men and women you had in mind when you entrusted them to our care. . . .

You will find the strength. For the way you look down on your sleeping children—with tenderest affection, desire for sacrifice—is the way God looks upon all of us, his children, all the time.

God will never leave your prayers unanswered.

Afterword

I WISH TO THANK the many great people who contributed, in one way or another, to the writing of this book.

First I thank my father and mother, James and Mary Stenson, who taught me so much about dedicated love with their words and splendid lives—lessons that have been with me now for more than half a century.

I thank Blessed Josemaria Escriva, the holy founder of Opus Dei, and his successor, the late and beloved Bishop Alvaro del Portillo. Their lives of sanctity and their lessons about the holiness of family life have directed the course of my life in countless ways.

Finally, I must thank those scores of valiant, good humored, adventurous parents who have shared with me their families' experiences through our many years of friendship. What I learned from them comprises most of this book. They are too numerous to name here, but this does not matter. They know who they are.

Index